Phil Scraton lectures in criminology and lives near Liverpool with Sheila Scraton and their two sons, Paul and Sean. His previous books include *Causes for Concern: British Criminal Justice On Trial?* coedited with Paul Gordon (Penguin, 1984) and *In the Arms of the Law: Deaths in Custody*, with Kathryn Chadwick (Cobden Trust, 1985).

Phil Scraton

The State of the Police

 Pluto Press

London and Sydney

First published in 1985 by Pluto Press Limited,
The Works, 105a Torriano Avenue, London NW5 2RX
and Pluto Press Australia Limited,
PO Box 199, Leichhardt, New South Wales 2040, Australia

7 6 5 4 3 2 1

89 88 87 86 85

Cover designed by James Beveridge

Phototypeset by AKM Associates (UK) Ltd
Ajmal House, Hayes Road, Southall, Greater London
Printed in Great Britain by Guernsey Press Co. Ltd.
Guernsey, C.I.

British Library Cataloguing in Publication Data

Scraton, Phil
    The state of the police.
    1. Police—Great Britain
    I. Title
    363.2′0941   HV8195.A2

ISBN 0 7453 0100 2

Contents

Acknowledgements

The State of the Police sets out to examine critically the politics of policing during the 1980s. It is rooted in the struggles of working-class people and their experiences of the police in their communities. It is not meant to be a definitive text on contemporary police work. There are many aspects of the daily routine of police operations which are not touched upon here. As a white academic I do not have to face the punishing experiences inflicted by white racist society, at its personal and institutional levels, on black people. Neither do I feel the bitter pain of being forced back to work by poverty and hardship which has been the experience in pit communities early in 1985. I experience daily, however, the consequences of what Stuart Hall termed the 'drift' towards a 'law and order society'. Since 1979 the police have shown forcefully that they are beyond the control of democratic government. The real price of that political autonomy has been paid in Britain's black communities and, in 1984, in the pit villages. *The State of the Police* provides a detailed explanation of how and why the crisis in British policing has emerged. It also aims to assess the consequences.

Working on a book such as this is often a harrowing, and rarely an enjoyable, experience. There are periods of real frustration and, sometimes, isolation. Many people have brought me through these periods and I want to thank them. Members of the Open University 'Crime and Society' Course Team provided a good deal of helpful and critical comment on my earlier work on the police. Stuart Hall, in particular, clarified my handling of the debates on police powers and accountability. Since 1982, workshop discussions with my criminology students at Edge Hill have contributed much to the book – particularly their comments on earlier drafts of some of the chapters. The original draft, however, has been improved markedly by the critical comments, friendship and support of Paul Gordon. Without Paul the book would not have been completed. At Pluto,

Richard Kuper first supported the project and Paul Crane has been a thorough, patient and understanding editor. Sheila Scraton has worked through many of the ideas contained in the book and has been a part of their development. Hilary Arnott, Kathryn Chadwick, Pat Craddock, Carol Johns, Martyn Nightingale, Susan O'Malley, Joe Sim, Tony Souza and Elaine Wade have provided technical help, criticism and, most of all, comradeship. Sally Channon typed parts of the final manuscript.

1. 'The best police in the world'

The coking depot at Orgreave, situated close to a small village on the outskirts of Sheffield in South Yorkshire, became front page news during the last week of May 1984. With the coal dispute into its fifth month, the Orgreave depot was the site chosen by the NUM for a mass picket which drew support from all British coal fields. As with the Saltley coke depot picket during the 1972 miners' strike, the intention was to close the depot and strengthen the dispute with a strong display of workers' solidarity. Neither the police nor the Tory government had forgotten the defeat at Saltley. Their sole aim was now to keep the depot open and inflict a real defeat on the union-backed picket.

On a warm summer day, against a backcloth of country fields and green trees, thousands of battle-dressed police officers lined up, truncheons drawn, behind a solid wall of riot shields. Suddenly, on the command of a senior officer, the wall parted and through the gap poured mounted police fully equipped in riot gear. As they charged through the fields they chased and truncheoned anyone in their path. The pickets, dressed mainly in summer clothes and training shoes, ran for their lives. After each charge the mounted police rode back through the ranks of the 'infantrymen' to the loud drumming of truncheons on riot shields.

The media reported the confrontation between 2,000 police and 7,000 pickets almost exclusively in terms of the violence of the pickets directed towards the police. *The Times* reported police allegations of barricades, battering rams and barbed wire traps for the horses. The *Daily Express* reported smoke bombs, thunderflashes, ballbearings and nail-spiked potato missiles. The *Daily Mail* added fencing staves to the list of weapons used against the police. The *Daily Telegraph* alleged 'bricks thrown at ambulancemen'.[1] Every newspaper quoted extensively from police sources, offering little or no analysis or alternative explanations from other eyewitnesses. The use of riot equipment and massed ranks of police was justified by the generalized accounts of exceptional levels of violence graphically written up in the daily papers.

According to the *Daily Mirror*, the 'job' of the police was 'to uphold the law and make sure the lorries got through'. *The Times* talked of an 'upsurge in violence' and quoted the Assistant Chief Constable of South Yorkshire, Tony Clement, as saying that the violent situation 'changes things'. In the *Daily Mail* his colleague, a Superintendent Pratt, argued that the 'unacceptable level of violence' required a positive response. Clement told the *Daily Telegraph* that it was the level of pickets' violence which had led to the 'use of riot gear, mounted police and dogs'. Any informed discussion or analysis of the police role in the lead-up to Orgreave, the operational policy decisions which put the police immediately on the offensive or the actual decisions to use offensive tactics on the day, was absent from the news reports. Questions of police powers and accountability, of training and practices in the use of riot equipment and of police intimidation or provocation were not even raised by most journalists.

The view of the pickets and of people monitoring the police role at Orgreave was quite different. Sheffield Police Watch, set up to monitor the policing of the coal dispute in South Yorkshire, stated in its report that three mounted-police charges on pickets occurred without provocation and that missiles were thrown by pickets after these charges despite appeals from NUM officials. It was the use of the horses that drew a violent response from some of the pickets. Pickets close to the ranks of riot police were arrested arbitrarily. One account of these arrests specifically alleges that there was a police instruction given over a loud hailer to 'take some prisoners'.[2] At this point the riot shields opened up and pickets were randomly pulled through the line. Many pickets arrested in this way complained of being beaten, kicked and dragged by the hair.

Following the random arrests on the line and well after the coke lorries had passed by, the riot police, both on horses and on foot, repeatedly charged the pickets. Penny Smith and Phil Thomas interviewed many of the South Wales miners who went up to the mass picket at Orgreave.[3] Their accounts state that the police baton charges came without warning and were directed at groups of miners who were standing around doing nothing. The numerous accounts, from miners throughout the South Wales coalfields, of the baton charges are horrifying. Likened to the Charge of the Light Brigade or to TV westerns, the mounted-police offensive was described as a brutal attack with anyone on foot taken as a legitimate target for batoning. People ran for cover to avoid being trampled by the horses only to be batoned by their riders. Further accounts state that the police used dogs in the offensive and that the police dogs were off their leads. Finally the police officers on foot were accused of 'dishing out instant justice'. Penny Smith and Phil Thomas concluded from their extensive interviews that, 'the scale of brutality is difficult to contemplate but it is important to remember that horses, dogs and paramilitary acted in concert'. It brought panic and mayhem with pickets chased into the village. Two quotes from Maerdy miners summarize the 'alternative version' of events at Orgreave:

I saw police throwing bricks from behind police lines. They were using truncheons, hitting men, charging horses, using dogs. I was petrified. We were in jeans, tee shirts, trainers, daps. They just attacked us. They let their dogs loose at us. I wish people could see a true picture of this. It was like a battlefield.

The most frightening and most violent picket was Orgreave. It frightened everyone. I've never seen anything like it in my life. The way the police acted towards us was really diabolical – it sickened me to watch it. I even felt violent myself and I've never been a violent person. I even threatened one, and this is something I thought I would never do to another human being, but the way they kicked me and hit me – you have to really experience it for yourself.

Whatever justification the police, the media or politicians put forward to explain the use of offensive and often brutal tactics at Orgreave the overwhelming impression left on miners and observers was that of an unprovoked, systematic assault on pickets regardless of their actions. They were legitimate targets simply by being there. There would be no stopping of the coke lorries, no closing of the depot and the pickets would be taught a severe lesson. It is this latter point which recurred in the pickets' accounts. They saw the police action as a well-organized offensive body geared solely to dishing out punishment to striking miners; a punishment which had its roots in the miners' victory at Saltley Gates. There would be no action replay at Orgreave.

Markham Main Colliery is situated at Armthorpe in the South Yorkshire coalfield. Throughout the first seven months of the miners' strike it had been a peaceful picket in keeping with good worker–management relations at a productive pit. On 21 August the solid strike was broken by three miners from outside Armthorpe. The hooded miners were 'escorted' to work by a police convoy and the four pickets on duty were knocked aside as the vehicles sped through the gates. The local NUM branch placed six pickets on the gate but during the night of 21 August more pickets arrived and alleged that police, sent to Markham from Greater Manchester, derided them by flashing ten-pound notes and hurling insulting comments. In order to ease the tension the NUM officials took away the pickets and the police removed five-sixths of their men.

By the time the police convoy was due at the pit a barricade had been formed across the pit entrance and apparently all police had been withdrawn from Armthorpe. Just after 8 a.m., without any warning or consultation, 52 transit vans filled with police officers in riot gear approached the pit in three columns. The police view[4] was that 'law and order' had broken down in Armthorpe and their intention was to 'retake' the pit gates and the entire village. The police strategy had been worked out carefully with columns of vehicles waiting to 'ambush' fleeing pickets as they ran from the initial police charge. Police officers in riot gear wore boiler suits concealing their numbers and chased pickets through the quiet village. They went through gardens, kicked down doors of houses, entered without warrants and swore at women who demanded to know why they had entered their houses. The accounts given by two of the women whose houses were entered are typical:

They were animals. They were hitting anyone they could find. I was once in favour of the police but there's no way they will get any help from me now. The back door was unlocked but they kicked it in. The police said, 'Send the bastards out.' I said, 'You're not getting in.' Then he jammed the door in my face. After that I could feel myself going.

I must have blinked because the next thing I knew, there was six riot officers in my kitchen. I was too frightened to do anything. I just stared. I then heard the window break. They caught up with one of the lads just outside my front hedge. There were six policemen and the lad they were chasing was on the floor. They were knocking hell out of him. Unless you have experienced it you could not believe it. I did not believe that police in this country carried on like this.

From the time of the police arrival to mid-afternoon Armthorpe was under curfew with all access to the community forbidden. A request made to a South Yorkshire inspector for an ambulance to be allowed in to pick up injured pickets was turned down by a more senior Greater Manchester officer who commented that injured pickets would receive all the attention they needed in police cells. The imposition of a curfew on the village of Armthorpe and the universal groundswell of public opinion throughout the community concerning the police tactics and brutality brought calls for a full public inquiry into the events of 21 and 22 August. Once again the most serious criticism levelled against the police was not individual acts of brutality but operational policy decisions, taken at senior level, which not only contributed to the confrontation but gave units of riot officers a license to go through the picket line and the village like a 'dose of salts'.

Questions of accountability, particularly the responsibility for the deployment and actions of officers from outside South Yorkshire, were also raised by Armthorpe. The lack of any consultation with the police committee over the use of offensive tactics and riot equipment was a further clear indication of the chief constables' disregard for local democratic accountability. As with Orgreave, the justification for the use of large numbers of riot police, truncheons drawn, was that law and order had broken down in Armthorpe. Though a barricade was constructed at the pit entrance, there was no substance in the allegation that a state of lawlessness prevailed. There was no mass picket and all was quiet in the village. Hostility towards the police, which is now universal in the village, had its origin in the tactics adopted by them. In a period of a few hours respect for the police and their version of law and order was lost in a community where there had been no violent confrontations or large-scale picketing.

Soon after the Armthorpe incident George Moores, the Chair of the South Yorkshire Police Committee, argued that with operational independence surrendered by local chief constables the coal dispute showed 'the creation of a paramilitary state police'.[5] In his opinion new recruits were being sent to police training school and leaving as 'storm troopers'. John Alderson, the former Chief Constable of Devon and Cornwall and a persistent critic of the drift towards aggressive and reactive forms of policing, commented on the Orgreave and Armthorpe incidents:

> For the first time we have seen the police having to resort to some kind of paramilitary style of policing which we have always associated with continental police forces and always prided ourselves in having avoided having to introduce.[6]

With the general application of riot training throughout UK forces and its ready deployment to 'trouble spots' on the basis of a nationally co-ordinated programme of 'mutual aid', Alderson considered that what has been instituted is a 'de facto national police force'.

This line of analysis is of primary significance in grasping the recent developments in the organization and management of policing in the UK. The danger is that the policing of the 1984–5 coal dispute will be interpreted as an exceptional response to an exceptional situation. The media, the police and politicians of all of the main parties balance the use of paramilitary strategies and practices against a naive acceptance of universal picket-line violence. It appears to be their assumption that now the strike is over, regardless of the outcome, British policing will return to 'normality' and the riot equipment will be mothballed until the next 'exceptional' situation demands its use.

This line of argument, which is used to justify real excesses at a range of levels in the policing of mining communities, denies the historical and political background to the debates around police powers and accountability. Thus the deployment of police beyond their own force boundaries (mutual aid), the purchase and use of varieties of 'riot equipment' and the operational priorities and strategies used by chief constables have all occurred without consultation with the appropriate police committees. For a society which makes so much of the issue of 'local' democratic policing this lack of consultation raises a major contradiction. What consultation has taken place has been between the Association of Chief Police Officers (ACPO), the Attorney General and the Home Secretary. With the Cabinet-based Civil Contingencies Unit monitoring and advising the Tory government and its Home Secretary on the best way of containing the pickets and breaking the strike, and with the National Reporting Centre (NRC) co-ordinating the entire police operation throughout the British coalfields, any effective political responsibility from local government was removed. It is of additional concern that the President of ACPO is automatically appointed as the NRC co-ordinator, and his role is to negotiate terms and decide on priorities for policing in direct consultation with the Attorney General and the Home Secretary.

These issues, discussed fully in Chapter 7, raise fundamental questions about the long-term preparation which has gone into policing industrial disputes since the miners' success in closing the Saltley Gates in 1972. Together with the emergence, growth and general acceptance of paramilitary training there has been a decade of development in policing industrial conflict and public order. Also significant, and on the agenda only since 1979, is the question of who controls the police and the debate about political accountability.

The events at Orgreave and Armthorpe – and these confrontations are but two of many other similar situations – pinpoint the central issue of the 'state of the police' in the mid-80s. In 1982, amidst controversy, the new face of modern policing was highlighted on Merseyside where, at a cost of over £9 million, the new 'Command and Control' headquarters was opened. It provides a level of professional and technological sophistication unique to police operations in the UK with a control room and computer suite designed by 'experts in the field of ergonomics'. What is significant about 'the most modern and well-equipped police headquarters in the world' is the way in which the police have traded the image of their role as being 'of the people'. The publicity brochure is headed by two quotes:

> The police of this country have never been recognized either
> in law or by tradition as a force distinct from the general

body of citizens. The principle remains that a police officer, in view of the common law, is only a person paid to perform, as a matter of duty, acts which, if he were so minded, he might have done voluntarily.[7]

There are two very important advantages that our police enjoy over most others in the world. Firstly, that it was founded on a tradition of common law – law that evolved naturally to meet the needs of the people – and, secondly, that its officers are drawn from the community, performing their duties on behalf of us all. The job of the police is therefore to uphold our own self-imposed rules.[8]

Thus the law is presented as a 'natural' form, emerging from the identifiable 'needs of the people'. The clear impression is that of a harmonious society with a consensual view on rules for the common good. The 'Law' is 'ours', the rules are 'self-imposed' and the police are *our* representatives in its neutral enforcement. This point is emphasized by the identification of the police with the community – acting on *our* behalf. This reflects a deeply held belief that the police are no more than 'citizens in uniform' engaged in 'policing by consent'. They are upholders of a just and consensual rule of law and they act as neutral arbiters in its enforcement. In large-scale confrontations the police provide the 'thin blue line' which keeps opposing factions apart.

For the police there is no contradiction between technological, managerial sophistication and the notion that they are 'of the community'. On the one hand, we have the presentation of the modern force as technologically refined and moving forward to meet the challenge of new levels of professional crime. On the other, the reassurance that the police remain the guardians of society's consensus. Senior officers constantly remind the public that they retain the confidence of most people in society; that they have a hard-earned reputation as the 'best police in the world'. The mask which perpetuates this imagery is a broad commitment to 'community policing'. As with Orgreave and Armthorpe, however, it is the police who define the operational boundaries, and, in their claiming of 'society's consent', it is they who create the consensual image.

Opinion polls record widespread support for and confidence in the police. For most people the principles of universally applied justice and equality before the law remain central to their idea of the criminal justice process. The media and politicians regularly pronounce that UK criminal justice remains the 'envy of the world'. Dutifully they acknowledge and then sweep under the carpet the Irish situation: special courts, special powers, armed police, an army of occupation and brutal methods of interrogation. Ireland's six northern counties are portrayed as an exceptional situation demanding an exceptional state response. This response, however, is not exceptional. 'Special' powers and 'special courts' have become so much a part of the administration of criminal justice in Northern Ireland that they are now 'normal'. Moreover, as foreseen by Frank Kitson, Army Chief of Staff in Northern Ireland during the early seventies, Ireland provides the training ground for the use of 'counter-insurgency' tactics' against other 'subversive elements'.[9] It is on this basis that special powers have been developed throughout the UK police forces and changes in the law promoted.[10]

Partly because most people leave school without any knowledge of legal practices, the law's derivation and its enforcement, and also because so much of what happens throughout the criminal justice process is either officially of professionally 'secret', popular myths about justice, fairness and impartiality persist. Wrapped in the language of patriotism, of being 'English', the process is defended. Occasional disclosures of police or judicial corruption, malpractice, sexism, racism and even brutality, are portrayed as aberrations in an essentially fair and just system.

Apart from Northern Ireland, people living in other UK inner cities, particularly blacks, tell different versions of the story of 'justice'. The specific targetting of identifiable groups by the police – the use of saturation tactics in neighbourhoods with large numbers of black people – has its roots in a long history of 'differential' policing. Such communities are not surprised by so-called special powers – they have experienced stop and search, arrest on suspicion, harassment and brutality for generations. The experiences of mining communities such as Armthorpe in 1984 are only extreme examples of strong forms of policing which have operated in Moss Side, Toxteth and Brixton for 30 years. It was these communities which demonstrated most clearly the oppressive nature of police operations during 1980 and 1981. And it was as a direct result of the police experience of these uprisings that paramilitary tactics, riot equipment and training became the dominant initiative in policing the eighties.[11]

Since the ideology of law and order is reinforced by an establishment media, these issues have moved very little beyond the communities involved. Not having any direct right of access to information, reporters are tied closely to police press officers for their stories. Wander in on an early-morning conference at any police headquarters and it is difficult to tell apart the givers and receivers of information. What arrives on the breakfast table or the mid-evening news has been through a gauntlet of police press officers, news reporters with vested interests to protect, editorial discretion and owners' policy. This gauntlet forms a fine sieve for our 'informal' knowledge of the police and the law. And it is at this point that an imaginary picture, as shown in the press coverage of Orgreave, becomes transformed into a generalized reality.

The State of the Police aims to provide a historical, structural and political framework for current developments in police operations and practices. How far is the 'acceptable face' of policing – Dixon of Dock Green – a media myth? Were the police readily accepted in the inner cities and towns of the nineteenth century? What has been the working-class experience of the police during unemployment marches, political demonstrations and on picket lines? Were the police trusted as fair, just and reasonable enforcers of an impartial law? How much has changed in the 1984 police response to the coal dispute as opposed to that of Tonypandy, the General Strike and the Northern Risings of the 1930s? These questions are central to the review of the development of the police in the next chapter. In Chapter 3 questions relating to police powers, discretion and accountability are considered in terms of the structure of the police embodied in statute and realized in professional, organizational practice. The issues raised here are taken up by a case-study analysis of the controversy over the policing of Merseyside between 1979 and 1983. It was the bitter struggle between successive Merseyside Police Committees and their Chief Constable, Kenneth Oxford, which first brought up the controversy over the political accountability of the police.

After the controversy over the police handling of black communities and the uprisings of 1980-1, the Scarman Report had a major impact both publicly and internally on the police. In Chapter 5 the debate around the Scarman Report is critically examined.

Here the denial by Lord Scarman that there was evidence of institutionalized police racism is important. This is followed in Chapter 6 by a discussion of the various proposals for legal and organizational change in the police which have been proposed since 1980. It focuses particularly on the defeated Bill proposed by Jack Straw MP which aimed to make the police more accountable, and on the passing of the Police and Criminal Evidence Act 1984. Also in Chapter 6 is a critical appraisal of the theory and practice of community policing and the pressure for the development of a national police force. Chapter 7 develops this point further by a critical account of the policies, priorities and practices adopted by the police during the 1984-5 coal dispute, which returns us to the fundamental questions raised by Orgreave and Armthorpe. The final chapter discusses the development of an effective political strategy of opposition to oppressive forms of policing. It considers the future of 'democratic' political accountability, and the significance of police monitoring as an alternative strategy.

2. The controversial tradition of the police

Some seem hell-bent on sacrificing a police style which is the envy of the world just because of a few hours madness on the streets. A hundred and fifty years of British police heritage down the drain. The official response in the aftermath of the rioting falls far short of the stimulus needed to achieve a worthwile solution . . . If we are to save ourselves from incessant conflict we must start talking hearts and minds, not CS gas and plastic bullets. We should be seeking to preserve our great tradition of policing-with-the-people and declare our abhorrence of the alternative now on offer. (Chief Constable John Alderson in a submission to the Scarman Inquiry 1981)

We would wish we could think that this was the only instance by which persons have met with their death by the villainous outrage of the police . . . But what right have the police to expect any other line of conduct from the police, when such, and other atrocities (little short of 11,000 charges) have been known to be committed, and no notice of them taken by the Secretary of State; who, when complaints are made, says he 'never interferes in the arrangements of the Metropolitan Police Force'. (Captain W. White on a coroner's jury verdict of 'wilful murder against a policeman unknown', 1833)

John Alderson, former Chief Constable of Devon and Cornwall, while opposing the shift towards the 'tooling up' of police forces, assumes that there is a tradition of public support and consent for policing in the United Kingdom. He shares this view of a natural heritage with others, like Sir Robert Mark, who argue that indiscretion or malpractices which occur from time to time are individual aberrations within an essentially just and fair system. White's account, just four years after the founding of the Metropolitan Police, indicates that such assumptions are seriously flawed. Recent critical work on the early history of the new police supports White's comment.[1] The Met. was then 'a power looked on by the masses with great mistrust: viewed, as it naturally was, as a military organization in the hands of the government,' which led to 'stubborn and protracted agitation' against them.[2]

Alderson's claim for the 'British heritage' of policing fails to examine the diversity of the police function and the diversity of 'public interest'. From the start the police had several different political dimensions: public order, crime, and industrial disputes. Each of these was governed by vested interests to which the police were expected to respond. Strikes, lockouts, demonstrations, riots and certain types of crime are about opposing interests. The side taken by the police in such confrontations is crucial in identifying them as the 'servants of public interest'. Clearly the police enforce public order as it is defined by the government or by employers and this raises the question of whose consent the police need and receive.

In this chapter the different political dimensions of police work, the tensions between senior officers and the state and the internal conflicts within the police are considered within the historical context. Alderson's claim for a British heritage free from conflict is challenged by an examination of the police role in public order and industrial conflict. How far was White's claim of the 'villainous outrage of the police' a teething problem? Did the police achieve acceptability, implying full consent, in *all* communities?

Public order: the early days

Police work, as we know it today, had its formal origins with the passing of the Metropolitan Police Act in 1829. Robert Peel, the Home Secretary at the time, is generally credited with the initiative of founding the 'new police'. At the time of the Act a full-time police force already existed in London to deal with control of the port and the city. The idea of a centralized and organized police force had long been debated. The 1829 Act was the turning-point for the earlier ideas of the Fieldings and Colquhoun.[3]

Outside the capital, however, communities had been policed by parish constables. The system of local appointments meant that local police were often committed closely to the interests of their local community. Foster's work on Oldham, for example, argues that the parish constables often worked under the direction of the local community.[4] The challenge to such partisan relationships came with the 1829 Act. Yet it was not until 1856 that the County and Borough Police Act compelled all areas to operate a full-time police force. So the first half of the nineteenth century was a period of haphazard and uneven development in police work. The lack of a centralized, national programme and the local autonomy of police forces are features that persist today although they are constantly challenged. The arrival of the new police was not a sudden, overnight occurrence. 'Unpoliced' towns and cities did not wake up one morning to find uniformed police on the streets operating a well-coordinated programme of law and order. The shift from the established system of parish constables to the institution of police stations, beat constables and priorities for intervention was gradual and spanned most of the nineteenth century. The transition to industrial capitalism during the late eighteenth century had changed the structural fabric of British society. There was at the same time a rapid growth in industrial towns and cities and a shift away from private forms of discipline in rural society. Inner-city deprivation, poverty and overcrowding were all closely linked to crime and the emergence of a 'criminal class'. The instructions circulated to the police in 1829 began by specifying the principal object of police work: 'the prevention of crime'.[5] Yet while the primary emphasis was on the rookeries and backstreets of London's underworld, the 'threat' of public disorder was tied to the 'threat' of crime. At the beginning of the nineteenth century workers had no right either to vote or form a union. The new working class of industrial capitalism was only beginning to organize for parliamentary and union representation.

The military was regularly entrusted with the state's authority to 'keep the peace', and often with devastating results. A parliamentary reform meeting in 1819 at St Peter's Fields in Manchester was dispersed by troops leaving 11 dead and over 150 with sabre wounds. During the earlier part of the nineteenth century the organized movements of Luddism (machine breaking and arson), Captain Swing (the protection of the customary rights of the agrarian poor), and Chartism (workers' rights under emerging capitalism), were controlled and regulated by the military. 'In the summer of 1812,' writes E.P. Thompson, 'there were no fewer than 12,000 troops in the disturbed counties'.[6] During 1842, at the height of Chartist activities, the government considered that the 'threat' touched every town and city in Britain. It was within this climate of civil disorder, culminating in the 1842 General Strike, that modern police work was initiated. The task of the police was to gain control of working-class communities who in their turn were committed to physical force and criminal acts in pursuit of their rights. The police also had to establish that civil disorders were matters for the civil police and not the military.

The new police were opposed from the outset and at various levels. Three parliamentary committees, in 1816, 1818 and 1822, rejected the 'police idea . . . as incompatible with British liberty'.[7] Only 11 years before the passing of Peel's Act, a parliamentary committee considered a police force would be 'a plan which would make every servant of every house a spy on the actions of his master, and all classes of society spies on each other'.[8] Almost immediately after the appearance of the police in London, local parishes demanded their abolition. A year after the Act, 'meetings of vestries all over London passed resolutions denouncing the new police as an "outrage and an insult" to the people'.

One of the most notable verdicts ever to be passed in a coroner's court occurred in 1833 at the inquest into the death of a policeman. He had died during a charge on demonstrators at a public meeting organized by the National Political Union on Cold-Bath Fields in London. The inquest jury returned a verdict of justifiable homicide indicating that the violent charge of the police deserved to be met with violence. This verdict was later quashed but has remained a measure of public resentment against and resistance to the early activities of the police at public meetings. For Critchley, regarded as an authoritative biographer of the police, this resistance represented little more than teething troubles. Almost as though public opinion had changed following the reversal of the inquest jury's verdict, he stated:

Such were the intolerable conditions in which the Metropolitan Police forged the reputation which, within a few years, was to make the force world famous. Their imperturbability, courage, good humour and sense of fair

> play won first the admiration of Londoners and then their
> affection . . . 3,000 unarmed policemen, cautiously feeling
> their way against a hostile public, brought peace and
> security to London in place of the turmoil and lawlessness of
> centuries.[9]

Thus, in Critchley's view, the new police gained the goodwill and represented the collective interests of the people within a decade of their establishment. Their presence on the streets, in his account, was well received in poorer communities as a challenge to inherent lawlessness and they represented an effective non-military challenge to regular civil disorder. The creation of an effective civil force can, however, be seen as representative more of the interests of the emerging state which allowed the military's more brutal episodes, such as Peterloo, to fade quietly into history.[10] Yet for Critchley, the new police were a non-political, state-sponsored force representing the common good and thus the 'neutrality' of the state's order. Without the vote or the right to form a trade union or strike working-class people did not consider the rule of law or the regulation of public order to be 'theirs'. The legal system had its roots elsewhere, reinforcing and protecting the structure of inequality.

The challenge to public order was most evident in the fast-growing towns and cities outside London. Civil disorder was the driving force behind the introduction of the new police in the provinces.[11] The provincial forces developed haphazardly and without any effective coherence. In his work Sir Leon Radzinowicz portrays the police as gradually being accepted, and even welcomed, nationally. Recent alternative accounts, however, challenge these assumptions.[12] These accounts document many violent and large-scale confrontations between the police and political demonstrators throughout the nineteenth century and show that some of the demonstrations were directed solely against the police and their powers. They argue that the police were most resisted when they attempted to restrict working-class traditions and recreational practices. Primarily intended to overview and regulate the activities of working-class communities, police action was bitterly resented and led to fierce confrontations.

The notion that the police were welcome in working-class communities is also questioned by recent careful documentation of confrontation in Lancashire and Yorkshire towns during the 1850s.[13] The police were regularly 'moving on' people who gathered on the streets. The freedom of assembly of the poor and working classes was challenged – police attempts to impose an authority on the streets had never previously been experienced. Local regulations concerning traditional recreations, such as drinking, cock fighting and street betting, were imposed in what was the emergence in northern towns of 'new standards of urban discipline'.[14] The resistance clearly was strong. One account concludes:

> Policemen continued to be beaten all through the nineteenth century for such reasons as interfering too closely in family or neighbourhood affairs, or public house proceedings, providing escorts for strike breakers, engaging in brutality, or moving people on too forcefully especially in times of high unemployment.[15]

The day-to-day relationship between people in working-class neighbourhoods and the policemen on the beat was thus determined by a range of factors. In Islington particular officers were remembered bitterly for their personal aggression.[16] It was at this time that the 'policeman' became synonymous with the evil threat of the 'bogeyman'.[17] Mistrust, according to these authors, ran deep. One account argues that it was founded on the generally accepted feeling that policemen had betrayed their class:

> Police, executors of laws made by others, were the objects of mistrust within working-class neighbourhoods. Few expected the police to do them any favours. Most memories are of the fear engendered by their presence . . . Because policemen were almost invariably from working-class backgrounds, their constant presence as an alien force within the working-class community smarted as a betrayal. Policemen clubbed strikers and sheltered blacklegs. Policemen worked while others went on the parish.[18]

It was this direct link between police action in working-class neighbourhoods and the deployment of officers against strikers which sharpened the resistance of working-class communities to police interventions. And it was the dual targeting of street practices and political agitation which laid the foundation for the relationship between the working class and the police. Another account reflects this point:

> In London especially, the metropolitan force was both the strong-arm and the advance guard of municipal reform. As a population formed by preindustrial and rural conditions crowded in and colonized the archaic urban infrastructure, it became less a question of enforcing their segregation from the upper classes than of policing their usage of social space and time so that it did not obstruct the traffic of industry and commerce. The potential sources of obstruction included not only strikes, political mobilization and organized crime, but also the development of street cultures and their irregular economies, upon which whole working-class communities came to depend as a means of local livelihood and identify against the anarchy of impersonal market forces.[19]

While it is also clear that in these neighbourhoods a police presence was requested, there is no clear indication of the criteria used by people when asking for police support or intervention.[20]

As the police continued to battle for control of working-class neighbourhoods, they were put under considerable political pressure to contain the 'threats' of the poor. The main source of official concern was the condition of the working class in the inner cities. In these communities, unemployment, casual work and extreme poverty laid the foundations for a real challenge to the established order. These conditions, inherited and seemingly unchangeable, left whole generations of people destitute. The struggle to survive under such wretched conditions either by crime or by spontaneous, violent demonstrations provided clear evidence to the upper classes and to the 'respectable' working class of the 'dangerousness' of the urban poor. While the reasons for poverty, crime and disorder were left unquestioned, the 'respectable' working class identified the unruliness and lawlessness of the poor as a real threat to their quality of life and its advancement. The unruliness of the poor threatened their ownership of property, small though it was, through crime. Strongly associated with this threat was the widely held belief that poverty was a contagious disease. The moral and physical degeneracy of the poor was portrayed as possibly contaminating to more respectable sections of the working class. The working class was thus split apart. On the surface the split was about 'the criminal classes' and their 'moral degeneracy' but the division was created by an expanding economy which maintained the bulk of its labour power as casual workers living in conditions of extreme poverty.

Explanations of and proposed remedies for the 'dangerous poor' had little to do with the causes of inequality and the creation of a reserve of casual workers necessary for the expansion of industrial capitalism. Nevertheless, street crime and theft obviously threatened *all* neighbourhoods and households which were relatively better off. If 'respectable' people were to be protected, then it was the poor who would have to be punished, corrected or, at least, saved. Prisons and workhouses were the vehicles of punishment which emphasized to individuals that their lot was their own fault. Other solutions, such as work camps, were also proposed as measures of correction but were directed primarily towards the 'collective' threat of the poor.

State responses to poverty, and those from charitable institutions or reform politicians, left intact the social and economic arrangements of the inner city which provided little or no opportunity for even a subsistence level of existence. The priorities of police work reflected this line in that they were directed against those sections of the working class considered to be 'rough' or 'dangerous'. It was the often violent struggle for the control of 'known' neighbourhoods which created the most significant barrier to the development of a police force based on consensus. The police represented particular interests, even within the working class. For just as certain sections of the working class, the 'respectable', sympathized with the containment of 'dangerous' elements in their communities, so they welcomed police strategies geared to that end. The police response was to fight violence with violence and punishments were immediate, personal and discretionary. In that sense a form of recognition was achieved as working people, for the first time, received protection from street crime and property theft.

The poor were also considered to have real potential as a political threat. While Chartism and the use of the riot receded during the second half of the nineteenth century, new threats to the state began to emerge. Unionism ceased to be the prerogative of craft workers and by the 1880s manual trades unions were making their presence felt. Political organizations were no longer preoccupied with parliamentary reform. Socialism, as a revolutionary alternative, had become a serious political development. The socialist movement gained significance and offered hope to the mass of casual workers who were underemployed and unemployed. The trade union movement became a very different organization once its doors were opened to the poor. This 'revolutionary potential' brought a new emphasis to police work.

In 1883 the Irish Special Branch was formed within the Metropolitan Police in response to the Fenian bombings in London during the early part of that year. Five years later, the bombings had stopped, but the new police unit stayed on as the Special Branch with the general brief to keep under close surveillance *all* potential threats to public order. The arrival of the Special Branch 'did not herald a new departure; it was the formalization and extension of previous practices'.[21] The involvement of the police with the threat of political and workers' organizations was not new and much of the provincial work continued to be handled by local CID officers (Provincial Special Branches were not set up till the 1970s). The development of surveillance and information gathering by the Branch along with new developments in detection, record keeping and fingerprinting provided the police with new scientific means of operation. Political groups which threatened public order were infiltrated and by the end of the century this practice was well institutionalized. The Branch had become a specialist force to deal with all serious forms of political agitation.

The idea that detective work should be a major part of preventive policing had been contested since the foundation of the new police. It was argued that the private affairs of individuals could be scrutinized and recorded without their knowledge. The techniques of surveillance represented a new departure in police work. Detective work required the involvement of third parties as informers. Surveillance brought the police into the negotiation of crime and political disorder *before* the events. Not only did this raise serious questions about methods of surveillance, such as infiltration, close involvement with informers and 'setting up', it also raised doubts about police powers and, inevitably, their accountability in these situations.

Thus the portrayal of the police as the 'thin blue line' or neutral arbiters in social conflict is naive. By the end of the nineteenth century the police had developed a clearly political function. In policing civil disorder, strikes and political demonstrations the police operated within parameters laid down by governments and interpreted by senior officers. This did not mean that in the course of specific events police officers did not possess discretion. Indeed, they possessed wide discretionary powers in the negotiation and enforcement of the law. Operational policies and priorities were of course influenced by governmental directives and popular opinion, but the police were at no point identified in working-class communities as being neutral either in their policy decisions or practices. As the enforcers of law and order they were engaged in the operation of a certain kind of law and order – one which never possessed the consent nor reflected the interests of the working class.

Assertions that the 'great achievement' of the nineteenth century was 'the elimination of riot from English social life . . . [by] the improvement of the machinery for enforcing the law'[22] should also be considered with care. The demise of the riot came from the involvement of the poor in unionism and new forms of political struggle rather than the effectiveness of the police. The relationship between working-class communities and the police was characterized by hostility and a 'grudging acceptance'.[23]

One bitter struggle for parliamentary reform was the fight for the women's vote. At the beginning of the twentieth century the state experienced the real threat of a move towards socialism and any further extension of rights to workers or citizens was clear evidence of that threat. The political demonstration provided the government with the opportunity to show that there would be no tolerance of the 'socialist' challenge and the police were expected to provide the first line of defence of the established order. Their handling of demonstrations followed central government instructions, often without consultation, and to many people the police were the only tangible experiences of the rule of the established order.

Women demonstrators were treated with exceptional roughness by the police and often worse by crowds. During the women's struggle for the vote it became clear that state institutions had developed a fully planned, coherent policy for handling the campaign. The punitive, public arrest of women by the police, their vicious treatment in prison and the passing of the 'Cat and Mouse' Act (used as a means of putting excessive pressure on the women's leaders by returning them to prison on release) constituted a deliberate attempt to break the movement. The police were used by the government as the first line of attack against a formidable and well-organized political movement. The idea that the police intervened against the suffragettes only as impartial enforcers of a fair law is a thin disguise for the level of brutality which campaigning women suffered at their hands.

Industrial conflict: between the wars

Miller's account of the relationship between the police and the working class[24] maintains that, with the exception of the handling of the suffragettes, the 'serious problems and criticisms' associated with the policing of public order and industrial conflict did not re-emerge until the late 1960s. He argues that by the twentieth century the police had become honest, impartial and non-violent – a fully fledged public service well adapted to the demands of political democracy. While there was a shift towards a 'grudging acceptance' of the police in the inner cities and industrial towns because they did often intervene in the interests of the poor, the bitter legacy was clear.

> The violence against individual members of the working
> class used by the state (through the police and the judiciary)
> in this process was without precedent in British history.
> How can the cumulative effect of thousands of arrests, trials,
> fines and imprisonments over many decades be adequately
> described? It was, in short, a process of attrition.[25]

Bolshevism seemed a real threat in a united and politically active working class. Its unity, coupled with growing unrest within the police service over wages, working conditions and the right to form a union, fuelled such fears. Both before and after the unemployment riots of the 1880s, in 1872 and 1890, the police had gone on strike for improved conditions and pay. Yet they continued to be used aggressively in the policing of strikes and demonstrations by the unemployed.

In 1910 Winston Churchill, then Home Secretary, sent the

Metropolitan Police to Tonypandy to deal forcefully with striking
miners. The strikers were subjected to baton charges and given 'a
little gentle persuasion with the bayonet' by the military.[26]

> The action of the authorities, especially its harshness at
> Tonypandy in 1910, can perhaps be explained in part by the
> fact that general labour unrest, seen by the government as
> the first tremors of Bolshevism, had seriously affected urban
> areas. Clydeside was in turmoil, as was Liverpool and much
> of the north of England . . . police at this time tactically
> knew no other way of tackling industrial unrest other than
> marching at it head on. The police were quite simply used as
> a battering ram in such situations. All their methods and
> training were aimed at strike-breaking rather than the
> impartial preservation of the public peace.[27].

A year later, in 1911, striking miners were shot in South Wales and
gunboats were anchored in the Mersey during the Liverpool
general strike. The police often found themselves caught between
the strikers and the troops. Yet in escorting blackleg labour, used to
break the strike, and in the baton charges against agitated strikers,
the police were part of a situation in which the troops inevitably
were used. The lead up to the Great War in 1914 produced an
'atmosphere of uneasiness, of disorientation, of tension'.[28] It was a
period 'of labour as an electoral force, of radicalization on the
socialist Left, of flaring bushfires of labour "unrest" [and] also
years of political breakdown'. [29] The war, then, was a respite from
crisis which, for a while at least, abated the threat within the nation.
After the war, however, the worst fears of the pre-war period
began to be realized. In August 1918 the police went on strike and
Lloyd George considered that the country was close to Bolshevism.
Clearly the civil force was necessary to combat the demands of the
workers:

> During the first three months of 1919 British capitalism was
> skating on thin ice. The 'revolutionary outburst' that was
> threatening in 1914 now seemed likely to materialize in a far
> more acute form and in circumstances vastly more menacing
> to the existing social order. Not only was the mass of the
> working class in a state of ferment; for the first time millions

of working men had been trained in the use of arms.[30]

On Clydeside the struggle for a reduced working week was gathering widespread support for a full strike. During a massive demonstration in central Glasgow the 'Battle of Georges Square' was fought. One of the strike leaders, Willie Gallacher, recalls that 'without warning of any kind a signal was given and the police made a savage and totally unexpected assault on the rear of the meeting, smashing right and left with their batons, utterly regardless of whom or what they hit'.[31] Such was the government's fear of a socialist uprising that the brutality of the authorities was a response to rumours of an imminent 'Spartacus coup' in Glasgow. The government dispatched troops 'lavishly provided with tanks and machine guns' to Clydeside in support of the police. Another account concluded: 'Everywhere men sensed that this was no ordinary strike and the authorities frankly feared a rising'.[32]

The impact of the revolution in Russia and the socialist movement in Europe gave credibility to the 'socialist threat'. Each series of disturbances was depicted in this context. The police, maintaining their uneasy alliance with the military, continued to provide the front-line containment of the threat. During 1920 the unemployed marched in London and once again 'were charged upon by the police . . . and beaten about by police batons, resulting in broken heads'.[33] In 1921 the miners were locked out by the colliery owners after the termination of state control of the pits, and a general railway and transport strike was threatened. A State of Emergency was declared by the government and the troops again brought in to 'resolve' a civil dispute: 'Machine guns were posted at pitheads. Troops in full battle order were despatched to the big working class areas'.[34]

With 2,000,000 people 'officially' numbered as out of work by mid-1921 the police were now clearly identified with the interests of employers. The relationship between the police and the working class was especially bitter during the General Strike of 1926.[35]

Baton charges sought to break up the mass pickets . . .
arrests mounted into the hundreds. In the 'state of
emergency' any form of strike activity could be, and was,
construed as an illegal act. Jail sentences rained down.[36]

Another account comments:

> Large numbers of arrests were made during the strike, often
> on the flimsiest of pretexts, and sentences handed down by
> magistrates little disposed to sympathy with those brought
> before them. There were numerous instances of baton
> charges by mounted and foot police against strike pickets
> and gatherings of strikers; and there was also a fair amount
> of licensed brutality on the part of volunteer special
> constables.[37]

The government also gave a mandate to the armed forces to pursue
'any action necessary' to aid the civil power. Once again the level of
force used was justified by the dual threat of political subversion
and the undermining of state security. The struggle for better pay
and against unemployment was redefined by the government as a
deliberate attack on the rule of law and democracy. Will Paynter, a
senior officer in the National Union of Mineworkers in the late
1920s, was highly critical of police methods and training at the time.
He argued that the strong links between the police and the
magistracy made it impossible to gain justice in the courts.[38]

The police were effectively given extended powers after the
General Strike. According to the Coles, the strike 'served as the
occasion for the enactment of a far more directly repressive
measure'.[39] This was the Trade Unions and Trade Disputes Act
1927. The Act made general strikes and strikes 'in sympathy' illegal
and circumscribed the right of picketing which had been given
some measure of status by earlier legislation. A new procedure of
injunction, used against trade unionism in the United States, was
also introduced. Finally, financial restrictions were imposed on the
unions.

Archaic legislation was revived to deal with so-called union
agitators. The 1817 Seditious Meetings Act was passed to prevent
meetings or demonstrations near Parliament. The police used the
1829 Police Act to break up political meetings on the grounds of
obstruction 'even where circumstances were such that there was no
traffic to obstruct'. Meetings near employment exchanges or at
well-established public meeting places were primary targets for
moving on assembled crowds.

The full impact of police powers and the use of the law is well illustrated by the 1932 Weavers Strike. The following is an account of a picket at Burnley, Lancashire:

> Never had such mass pickets been seen; thousands of strikers rallied on the streets leading to the few mills which endeavoured to keep working . . . the whole atmosphere became electric . . . hatred for the employers, and fierce contempt for the knob-sticks [blacklegs] . . . From the beginning of the Burnley strike, police were imported by the hundreds . . . Baton charges were an everyday affair. Young and old, women and girls as well as men were clubbed . . . Typical was the battle between a mass picket of 5,000 and a large force of police outside Hargher Clough mill. In a baton charge many workers were injured and several arrests made; but the workers fought back, injuring one policeman and releasing some of those arrested. The Trade Disputes Act 1927 was constantly invoked. To be out on picket at all, even to boo, was sufficient for charges of obstruction, disorderly behaviour and assault.[40]

Throughout the north of England police fought running battles with strikers and unemployed protestors. The situation on Merseyside was critical. Between 1930 and 1932 unemployment had more than doubled in some areas. In Birkenhead the registered number of women and men out of work was 36.2 per cent of the work force. Almost half of all male workers received welfare relief.[41]

> . . . for most this meant having to succumb to the means test administered by the PAC, the body which had taken over from the Poor Law Guardians. The economy measures introduced by the national government the previous autumn heralded the arrival of the means test. Soon the sight of the 'means test man', the relieving officer, visiting houses, quizzing, recommending how to live, hoping to catch out those with sons or daughters maybe working for a few bob a week, became a common sight . . . In five out of every six cases payments were reduced. Hunger and starvation closed in.[42]

As a result of these heavy-handed methods the National

Unemployed Workers Movement leadership called for a national 'mass struggle' on the streets. The idea was to put 'tremendous pressure' on the locally administered Public Assistance Committees by public demonstration, using force where necessary. In Birkenhead the 'mass struggle' ensued with thousands of demonstrators marching on the town hall. The police erected barricades to prevent assaults on local authority officials and councillors and this led to open conflict between the police and the marchers. The pressure brought results and the council voted against the operation of the means test, but the real struggle remained – the Public Assistance Committee had to be convinced.

Two days after the council success over 12,000 women and men marched on the PAC offices. All they were given was a promise of reconsideration of the case against the means test. They marched to the houses of some of the Tory councillors. The crowd was charged repeatedly by the police, fighting continued long into the night and the local Chief Constable took over the operations. By the early hours of the morning 37 civilians had been hospitalized, 'mostly with head injuries'. Throughout the week, rioting continued. The police response had resulted in a full-scale conflict between them and the poor of the town. As the police walked through streets of tenements they were showered with 'wash basins, bricks, flat irons and full bed-pans'. The street battles continued throughout the weekend – the rioting had been persistent for almost a week. On Sunday night the police decided that the offensive tactics of the street should be taken right into the tenement homes. The following is an account of the police offensive:

About 1.30 a.m. we were all fast asleep in bed, having had no sleep the previous two nights . . . We were all awakened by the sound of heavy motor vehicles, which turned out to be Black Marias. Lights in the houses were lit, windows opened to see what was going on. Policemen bawled out 'lights out' and 'pull up those fucking windows'.

Hordes of police came rushing up the stairs, doors smashed in, the screams of women and children were terrible. We could hear the thuds of the blows from the batons. Our doors were bashed by heavy instruments. My husband got out of bed without waiting to put his trousers on and unlocked the door. As he did so 12 police rushed into the room, knocking him to the floor, his poor head split open, kicking him as he lay. We were all in our nightclothes. The language of the police was terrible. I tried to prevent them hitting my husband. They then commenced to baton me all over the arms and body. As they hit me and my Jim, the children (five of them) and I were screaming and the police shouted, 'Shut up, you parish-fed bastards'.[43]

The assaults on the working-class communities in Birkenhead were arbitrary and vicious; moreover, the police secured considerable convictions in the courts on their evidence alone. The judiciary dealt with the more serious charges of riot, handing down sentences of hard labour and making claims that the riots had been 'deliberately engineered' by subversive elements seeking to capitalize on the situation. The police had been allowed a free rein not only on the streets but in administering their own vindictive punishments within the community.

The events on Merseyside were not unique. Apart from being repeated in other northern towns and cities, aggressive, forceful tactics became routine in policing the hunger marches.[44] Again the actions of the police were upheld in the courts and approved by government. The Home Secretary stated in 1932 that the communists were the 'prime instigators' of the marches and that plans for them were 'subordinated for their purpose'. The partiality of the police became a source of considerable bitterness with the emergence of British fascism in the early 1930s and what Tom Bowden calls the 'ostentatious protection' [45] given to their marches. The issues are reflected by the following observation:

It is impossible, in the light of recent happenings, to acquit the police and the courts of bias in the handling of different types of political offenders. The workman, who, probably after bitter experience of prolonged unemployment, is accused of 'seditious' utterances, goes easily to gaol; the gentlemanly young Fascist, who makes a boast of violence and swaggers about trying to induce race hatred and pogroms against the Jews, is usually let off with a caution.[46]

Little was done by the Home Office or Senior Police Office to control the fascist movement which contrasted starkly with the violent handling of pickets, unemployed marchers and anti-Mosley demonstrators. Undoubtedly, as personal accounts testify,[47] individual police officers were often in sympathy with Mosley's fascists. The 'threat' posed by socialism and workers' movements received the highest priority. The poverty of the towns and cities, aggravated by hard-line employers and governments without any welfare commitment, created the conditions of political struggle. The severe and persistent response of the police in that struggle aligned them with those employers in the minds of the workers. In using the law to maintain order the police were part of that establishment.

Crime and the 'criminal class'

Research by Jennifer Davis on north London police operations in Islington shows that by the last quarter of the nineteenth century the police carried a very clear image of what constituted *the* 'criminal class'.[48] Rather than focusing their attention on those people who had the best opportunity to commit crime – those in work – the police primarily monitored the unemployed or casually employed poor. The imagery of the 'criminal class', the 'rough' and the 'dangerous' – if you are not born bad you will soon catch it – became the excuse for concentrating police resources within certain areas. Davis shows that the police lost no time in establishing useful sources of information and pinpointing so-called problem families. From these first attempts at identifying the 'criminal class' and targeting particular people it has remained difficult to establish how far the claimed high incidence of crime in such areas is a product of high levels of police operations.

While it is difficult to trace the precise relationship between economic conditions and criminal activity, some writers, such as Herbert Mannheim, have shown that during the interwar period there were close links between crime and unemployment.[49] Yet Mannheim's work contains a warning against taking criminal statistics at face value. He argues that changes in the methods of and criteria for reporting, recording and prosecuting adopted by the police throughout the interwar period had a significant bearing on the apparent incidence of crime. As we have seen, the priorities adopted by the police clearly have an impact on how criminal activity is perceived in any given period. What appears to be the most regularly committed crime might be that which is most regularly reported, consistently recorded, or selectively policed. Changes in the definition or, as happened in 1932, the registration of crime can dramatically influence the statistics.

In establishing that unemployment constituted an 'overwhelming force' as a 'crime-producing agency' Mannheim went further than a simple statistical correlation. He researched official accounts and reports which established that a combination of long-term unemployment and a reduction in unemployment benefit in 1921 left the unemployed demoralized – none more than the youth of the inner cities. Young people left school at 14 to face, at best, casual work with very low wages in appalling working conditions. If they were employed on a regular basis they could expect to be laid off as they approached the age when full rates of pay applied. The 1930s brought a hardening of these conditions and a climate of despair. Mannheim concluded that 'a very considerable part of the total crime rate was due to unemployment'. Other writers, such as the historian Gatrell, argue that the relationship between economic recession and increases in crime was so marked that the authorities took it for granted that during hard times theft would escalate.[50]

Unemployment duing the interwar years forced whole communities into poverty, particularly in the north of England. Already depressed areas experienced a deepening of the effects of poverty. The jerry-built, back-to-back ghettoes of the industrial revolution deteriorated in stark contrast to new developments housing the wealthy. Within the cities and towns the resentment of material deprivation after the First World War not only inspired class-based political action but also a range of criminal activity. Street economies and 'craft'-based crime continued to develop, but these activities were supplemented by gang-based activities.[51]

The explanation for the emergence of gangs – assumed to be young, male and violent – was crudely 'evil work for idle hands'. Taking their collective identity from their specific neighbourhood, gangs were characterized by their bitter and hostile rivalry. Street fights were seen more as a public order problem than as a 'crime' problem. Warfare between gangs, however, was only part of the story. Breaking and entering, theft and small-scale protection provided gang members with a necessary income; they were in fact highly organized and had a tradition of carrying and using weapons.[52] According to James Patrick, the gangs in Glasgow had their origins in the 1880s, were not exclusively male, paid levies, held membership cards and looked after the dependants of married men sentenced to gaol.[53] Sir Percy Sillitoe, who was appointed as Chief Constable specifically to deal with the 'gang problem' in the 1930s, adopted a response to Glasgow's gangs which was based on the belief that hooliganism was inherited – they were simply a bad lot. Patrick's account provides a different picture. The gangs were subjected to 'appalling housing conditions' and had become 'inured to both evils, to cramped verminous houses and to brutal, barbarous violence'. His account relies on environmental explanations particularly in discussions of territoriality, drunkenness and street violence. Other writers, and accounts of those such as Patrick Meehan and Jimmy Boyle who grew up in these communities, show that the gangs provided the foundation for more organized criminal activities such as house breaking, bank robbery and protection.[54] While it is important not to overemphasize the ties between youth gangs and organized crime, there is a good deal of evidence to show that links did exist. Youth gangs did at least give to their members an initial, albeit petty, grounding in crime on a collective basis.

Jimmy Boyle's account of his youth in Glasgow stresses the organization of the gangs, their sound base for stealing from lorries and shops and their relationship to the real, adult and craft-based crimes such as safe blowing. The shebeen or illegal drinking house was the focus for the street economy of stolen goods, prostitution and gambling.

Glasgow was not the only centre for the development of professionally organized criminal gangs. Most large towns and cities in Britain had similar gangs. In Liverpool prostitution was organized and controlled by professional gangs, and this was extended in other cities to robbery, burglary, vice rings and protection rackets. In London and Birmingham well-organized gangs ran gambling and bookmaking. It is clear from a range of accounts that the war provided an unprecedented opportunity for the development of organized crime.[55] The scarcity of all kinds of commodities and the rationing of food opened the door wide for growth in the black market. People who usually would not steal became regular clients of black marketeers. Patrick Meehan tells his story, with some satisfaction, of selling black market clothing coupons to 'the wealthy ladies of Glasgow'.[56] The black market operation soon blurred the lines between the legitimate and the illegal business operation. There were considerable profits to be made from scarcity and, as David Yallop comments, 'many a middle-aged businessman owes his present successful position to the judicious buying and selling he did in those postwar years'.[57]

Another account of the immediate postwar years shows that black market rackets continued to develop, encouraged by the growing numbers of returning servicemen, deserters and young unemployed.[58] Most of these people were amateurs, becoming involved in regular, small-scale crime for the first time. The climate and organization of more serious crime, particularly theft, underwent some changes. Reported indictable crime rose dramatically in the postwar period. Steve Chibnall quotes the figures for 1947 as being 50 per cent up on 1939 with reported robberies with violence running at three times the prewar rate. [59]

In the postwar period two well-established criminals, Billy Hill and Jack 'Spot' Cromer, joined forces to control London's West End underworld of large-scale protection rackets, gambling and prostitution. This period saw the serious development of corrupt relationships between police and organized crime. Following a breakdown in the Hill-Cromer alliance in 1955, during which a full-scale American-style gang war was narrowly averted, the control of London's West End crime was left to a range of smaller gangs with no apparent central direction. Into this obvious opening moved the Kray brothers who refused to make deals with other gangs or with the police. They opened a West End-style club in the East End and, with the aid of well-known celebrities and business people, presented a front of respectability. At the same time, other gangs such as the Richardsons emerged. The popular image of the postwar gang has been that of ruthless, violent and often vicious thuggery. Yet, as Mannheim shows, this was only part of the picture. Gangland activities continued to demand the 'co-operation between a mixed strata of society'.[60] Indeed, the line between respectability and unlawful business has always been difficult to draw. What is also consistent throughout the accounts of this period, particularly from those directly involved, is that crime was a conscious choice as a 'career' or profession.[61]

The postwar 'crime wave', then, was seen as developing on two levels – working-class street crime and organized professional crime. As far as the police were concerned, certain neighbourhoods still housed the criminal classes where crime was part of a way of life. One writer suggests that areas such as Bethnal Green in East London were patrolled warily, 'generally in twos', and most detective work was restricted to recovering stolen goods.[62] Day-to-day conflicts, such as fights, were left mainly to the community to regulate. What emerged from this period was an unwritten agreement between the police and working-class communities based on levels of 'acceptable' crime – a blind eye being turned to street trading, the handling of stolen goods and most acts of male violence. This set the terms of the negotiation of law enforcement between the police and local communities.

The police response to organized, professional 'gangland' crime was quite different. The 1960 Gaming, Betting and Lotteries Act encouraged the development and expansion of the casino industry and contributed further to the opportunities for organized crime. The criminal activities of Britain's postwar gangs did not develop in a syndicated form, involving police and judges, as is common in the USA. Having said that. gangs operated clearly defined businesses in pornography, drugs and money lending and this included the buying off of the police in a big way.[63] Within a short period the Metropolitan Police CID was hand in glove with organized, professional crime. During the late 1950s the 'big hit' bank and payroll robberies, lorry highjacks and burglaries emerged. These crimes demanded careful planning and arrangement. By the 1960s bank robbery had replaced the craft of safeblowing with violent, fast-moving hold-ups using surprise, guns and getaway cars. The 'hit and run' tactics of big robberies changed the face of the organization of crime. Careful preparation, often relying on inside tip-offs, required the involvement of many people. Wider knowledge of planned crimes meant that it was possible for the police to gain access to their planning and organization through cultivating informants. Informants were put on the police payroll.

Another result of changes in organized crime was that large-scale business corporations and banks – the victims of big robberies – encouraged the development of new forms of protection. The armoured transport of payrolls, cash or valuables led to a further escalation in the violence of gangs, particularly the use of guns.

In August 1963 the build-up of well-organized and often violent robberies of cash in transit came to a head with the Great Train

Robbery. A mail train from Scotland to London was robbed of 2½ million pounds in non-traceable banknotes. If the police could make early arrests, their dealing with known criminals and paying for information would be justified. Within two months of the robbery five of the gang were in custody, the police had evidence against another five and the names of a further four. The negotiations extended beyond deals for information to deals over the evidence itself – a strategy which soon became part of the regular framework for policing serious crime.

The appeal judge's comment captured the 'crime war' mood of the period. He described the robbery as 'organized banditry', 'an act of warfare against the community reaching new depths of lawlessness'. Sentences ranged from 20 to 30 years – shots across the bows of organized crime. This outcome vindicated the use of cash payments by the police and the trading of evidence for information. It was a formal opening and official recognition of undercover dealing in which the end was seen to justify the means. One account argues that many people defined the police as 'oppressive, hypocritical and cruel' and concludes:

> The picture of the Metropolitan Police which emerges from
> the Train Robbers' story – some of them taking bribes to
> alter evidence or drop charges, and others fabricating
> evidence to secure convictions – may well be exaggerated,
> but because so many Metropolitan Police officers have been
> convicted of corruption or dismissed from the force since
> the Train Robbery took place, it cannot be regarded as
> totally false.[64]

The police and the courts were under pressure, both from the media and from Parliament, to gain convictions by whatever means possible. There was also considerable pressure within the police to specialize police operations and establish new technologies to prevent the expansion of organized crime. Surveillance through informants was one such development and this close contact with well-known criminals was to become the most useful means of securing convictions. Soon it became apparent that the police were not only negotiating for information with organized gangs but also had become involved directly in their activities. They were, to some extent, living off the proceeds of large-scale crime.

With the conviction rate the only public measure of the success of the 'war on crime', the police were regularly accused in the 1960s of heavy interrogation, violence, 'fitting up' and the actual setting up of robberies. At best it was becoming increasingly clear the police bent the rules designed to protect people detained under suspicion. This was, to some extent, eventually confirmed in Sir David McNee's evidence to the 1980 Royal Commission on Criminal Procedure (the RCCP). His evidence, given when Metropolitan Commissioner, stated that the police had learned to use 'stealth and force illegally'. Because people were becoming more aware of their civil rights he concluded that it was becoming increasingly difficult for the police 'to bluff their way into obtaining consent to take body samples, or enter premises illegally'. His solution to this 'embarrassment' was to propose to the RCCP the removal of many of the rights of protection afforded to suspects or detainees.[65]

McNee's predecessor, Sir Robert Mark, had noted the level of police involvement with organized crime.[66] The liaison between officers and known criminals and the exchange of money, information and evidence was apparently rarely scrutinized. Mark maintained that the problem was so serious in the Criminal Investigation Department that their work required review and reconstruction. Drastic measures, including the dismissal or resignation of many officers and the institution of a new internal investigations department, were essential. There were several hundred dismissals or resignations, and a new internal investigations department – A.10 – was established at Scotland Yard to police the Metropolitan Police. Eventually this led to a major investigation of police corruption – the ill-fated 'Operation Countryman'.

The public revelation of these allegations of widespread corruption, given credibility by Mark's actions and by convictions in the courts, created an internal struggle within the Metropolitan Police and made public an issue – police corruption – which had long been denied. The handling of the issue of corruption by Mark, his institution of A.10 and his 'struggle for control of the CID' was used by the police as clear evidence that the police could effectively police themselves. As far as they were concerned the 'crisis' was over. In the long term, however, the effectiveness of these internal investigations, particularly the notable overall lack of Countryman's success, shows that corrupt practices persist and are not effectively controlled.

By the mid-1970s, despite Mark's public purge of the CID, the close relationship between the police and organized crime had become institutionalized in a quite different form. Negotiations between members of the Robbery Squad and an informant, Bertie Smalls, with regard to a series of bank robberies between 1968 and 1972, heralded the arrival of the 'supergrass'. Smalls was housed, paid expenses and given immunity for his past crimes, except murder, in return for detailed information on the robberies which would lead to convictions. This was a considerable coup for the police. It cleared up a series of serious crimes but, more significantly, it struck deep into the confidence of those involved in organized crime. The 'trust among thieves' had been challenged and was in ruins. Once this inroad had been made by the Robbery Squad the traditional mould of detective work had been broken. As McNee has since stated, 'an extensive and updated intelligence network' coupled with the development of supergrass policing brought 'major successes and a significant reduction in the number of armed robberies'.[67] Yet supergrass policing has not been achieved without opposition. Lord Justice Lawton, for example, showed concern over the Smalls' precedent. He hoped that 'we will not see the undignified sight of the Director of Public Prosecutions making agreements with professional criminals again'. What has happened since is in direct contrast to those sentiments. By 1979 criminal investigation had become well adapted to supergrassing and although Lord Justice Roskill considered it to be 'unethical' he felt that it was an essential weapon against violent crime.

In his autobiography, Maurice O'Mahoney tells of giving information to the police on more than 200 people which resulted in 20 convictions.[68] He received a lesser sentence and was 'looked after' by the police on his release. The regularity with which supergrasses were being used, together with claims that the police and informants were involved in 'fitting up' people for crimes they did not commit, contributed to the setting up in 1978 of Operation Countryman. The debate was fuelled by further revelations of direct police involvement in organized crime.[69] Allegations made to Operation Countryman included detectives actually setting up and keeping the uniformed police away from robberies. Further to these claims were

. . . steering inquiries away from the real culprits to innocent men; helping criminals to get bail; deliberately offering feeble evidence in some cases; framing criminals in others by planting evidence such as shotguns and 'verballing'.[70]

Verballing, the construction of confessions by the police, has involved not only serious crime but also a whole range of quite ordinary cases. The full extent of the Operation Countryman inquiry is not clear. Although it eventually secured some convictions in 1982, if convictions of corrupt officers is the yardstick of success, its overall investigation was a failure. Its senior officers have stated publicly that they came across hostility and obstruction from the Met. during the investigation and a marked reluctance by the DPP to prosecute officers under suspicion. What remains at issue is the close association of the police with known criminals and informants, particularly the question of supergrasses. These developments show that unacceptable and illegal practices are now deeply institutionalized, justified by the need to provide convictions in the 'war on crime'.

In this chapter it has become clear that in a whole range of situations the police have immense discretion in defining, convicting and sentencing. They are central definers, by their actions, priorities and selective interventions, of crime in society. The well-established history of identifying and targeting working-class criminal neighbourhoods is the cornerstone of their operations against most crime. 'High crime neighbourhoods' which house 'the criminal class' are those most heavily policed. Identifiable groups, particularly blacks, are too easily and readily associated with certain types of crime. This has been particularly the case with street crime. The concentration of resources in working-class neighbourhoods, particularly using special squads to 'clean up' specific areas, has not only done much harm to good police-community relations but has also ensured that many other forms of crime in more 'respectable' communities go unpoliced.

As with the discussion on public order and industrial conflict, differential policing of crime raises important questions about the class interests served by contemporary police work. The historical evidence clearly identified the police as an oppressive force working against the communties from which their members were recruited. This appears to be still the case – with the notable, and significant, exception of their contribution to the oppression of black communities.

The response to professional and organized crime, however, raises questions of a different order. These centre on police involvement in obtaining information, their direct interference in the working of the courts, through plea-bargaining, and their manipulation and control of evidence. The justification for 'cutting corners', abandoning civil liberties and 'leaning heavily' on suspects is the need to secure convictions against those involved in serious crime. What emerges from the recent developments not only centres on police involvement in criminal operations – but also where, when and who draws the lines of operations.

This chapter has shown that commonly held assumptions that the police have a well-established history of policing by consent is a myth. The 'great tradition of policing with the people' referred to by John Alderson in the opening paragraph has little substance. Within working-class communities the effectiveness of crime control by the police throughout the nineteenth and twentieth centuries depended mainly on the success of officers on the beat to 'agree terms' with the people whose neighbourhoods they patrolled. The eventual grudging acceptance of the police in these neighbourhoods was a long time coming and resistance has persisted, repeatedly erupting into street confrontation.

Much of the quality of police-community relations has depended on the police response to the communities. The police were accepted in small town neighbourhoods and villages more readily than in the larger towns and inner cities. They played an important part in the definition and construction of reputations of criminality and violence. Their targeting of the 'criminal classes', with its origins in late nineteenth-century forms of regulation, surveillance and control, has done much to create persistent tension between particular communities and the police. This is not to ignore the fact that crimes against property and crimes of violence occur in working-class communities and that poorer people are also victims of such crimes.

What is clear, however, is that the police have not developed strategies for meeting the needs of policing working-class communities and have dismissed demands for effective policing – against racial attacks, sexual attacks, burglary – as exaggerated claims from people who, because of their class position, should expect to live with the consequences of 'inevitable' criminality. These tensions have been particularly marked in the inner cities where whole areas, and therefore the people in them, are written off as 'slags' or 'scum'. These issues, particularly with regard to racism and the police response to black communities, are dealt with in later chapters.

Where the police have most vividly come up against the working class, and where the explicit mistrust of their role has been most sharp, has been the policing of public order and industrial conflict. On these issues the historical evidence is overwhelming. The poor and unemployed, workers on strike, and political demonstrators have always represented a threat to the established order. Working-class resistance to poverty, unemployment, casual labour and so on – struggles against the persistence of exploitation – has been met directly, on the streets or the picket lines, by the police as the state's civil force of regulation and control. This has placed the police against working-class interests, and in their enforcement of the law against hunger marchers, political demonstrators and strikers they have been identified with employers and oppressive governments. There has furthermore been an institutionalization of aggression towards marchers and pickets. The police have thus become closely identified, both in operational policies and practice, with interests opposed to the political interests of the organized labour movement. The organized working class have never accepted the police role in strikes or lockouts, and the police have come to represent middle and upper class interests in British society. Chapter 7 takes this issue further with an analysis of the policing of industrial conflict during the postwar period.

3. The crisis in police accountability

On 14 January 1983 at 6 p.m. Metropolitan Police officers opened fire on a Mini which was caught up in rush hour traffic. Fourteen shots were fired at or into the car. The three people in the car, a woman and two men, heard no warning. The driver, Steven Waldorf, was seriously wounded and nearly died. It was, said the police, a case of mistaken identity. The officers had thought that Steven Waldorf was David Martin, wanted for a series of serious charges including attempted murder. Waldorf was implicated by travelling with Sue Stevens, a close friend of David Martin. For several days, as Waldorf fought for his life, the story was headline news. There was an immediate outcry over the use of arms by the police.

Soon after the shooting two officers were charged with attempted murder. Waldorf began a gradual recovery and comment on the case began to quieten. At their trial the officers – Finch and Jardine – were found not guilty of attempted murder. Police press officers and politicians sought to defuse the issues raised by the affair by pointing out the difficulties faced by the police dealing with hardened, armed criminals. David Martin, it was announced, was such a person. The concern over the use of firearms and the dramatic situation in which the shooting of Steven Waldorf took place put the Home Secretary, William Whitelaw, under considerable pressure. Within two months he responded with new guidelines on the use of guns by police officers.

The guidelines stated that guns should be used by properly trained and authorized officers only as a 'last resort' following the failure of more 'conventional methods'. They also instructed that the power to issue guns should be restricted to senior officers only. It appeared that the Home Secretary, as the definer and protector of the 'public interest', had responded quickly and firmly to the serious criticisms generated by the shooting of Steven Waldorf.

Questions concerning the status of the guidelines, the relationship between the Home Secretary and chief constables in matters of operational policy and the role of police authorities in serious decisions such as the use of arms, were immediately raised. On 5 April 1983, only weeks after the publication of the Home Secretary's guidelines, Greater Manchester's Chief Constable, James Anderton, provided the answer. He announced that 'armed police officers, travelling in signed police vehicles, are patrolling Greater Manchester round the clock to deal with a serious escalation of armed robberies'. He gave no indication of the number of officers involved. Neither the leader of the Greater Manchester Council nor its police committee had been consulted about this unique development in British police work.

Anderton's decision to arm a unit of patrolling officers on a round-the-clock basis (he qualified his statement a day later when he claimed that it was a 'temporary measure') flew in the face of the Home Secretary's new guidelines. Whitelaw's definition of 'last resort' had been stretched beyond recognition. The Home Office was immediately asked for clarification of this new development. The response was the unambiguous statement that the arming of the police remains an operational policy matter solely at the discretion of chief constables and their assistants.

The outcry over arms was the most dramatic example of the growing opposition to police strong-arm tactics and authoritarianism. It fuelled controversy over the operational policy decisions of senior officers – which includes their priorities for law enforcement – through to the operational practices adopted by the police officers responsible for the enforcement of these priorities. While the shooting of Waldorf and the arming of a unit of the Greater Manchester Police are only tenuously linked in terms of the issue of guns, they are significant because they reflect, albeit at different levels, the discretionary powers possessed by the police. Just as a chief constable's decision put armed police on the streets of Manchester, so an operational decision was taken to arm Metropolitan officers in the hunt for David Martin. Once these *policy* decisions had been taken, the use of arms rested with the lawful discretion and professional judgement of the officers assigned to particular cases.

The relationship between operational policies and operational practices is most important in considering the issue of police accountability. It can be seen in stark relief in the accounts of police operations at Orgreave and Armthorpe given in Chapter 1. The issues raised by these accounts relate both to policing strategy as planned at a senior level, and to the attitudes and behaviour of the officers who put that strategy into practice. At both levels the police are given broad discretion. The extent to which boundaries are set to that discretion represents the limits of effective police accountability.

In principle the boundaries are set at three levels. First, as senior police officers constantly remind their critics, there are the legal constraints on the actions of police officers. The police are 'citizens in uniform' and are subject to the rule of law in exactly the same way as any other citizen. Second, there are organizational constraints. Every police force operates a code of discipline which covers a broad range of issues relating to the conduct of officers. Many of these issues would not be unlawful but would fall below the standards laid down by the force. Finally, there are political constraints. These relate to the political powers of the Home Secretary and the local-government-based police authority (usually termed the police committee of the local authority). The important issue here is the relationship of central and local government to the chief constables.

The first part of this chapter discusses the legal and organizational constraints on the discretionary powers of the police. In the second part the formal structure of political accountability is outlined.

Police powers and the fine line of discretion

The demand for police accountability appears straightforward: provide a code of conduct, set up a procedure for handling complaints, and at all levels make the police responsible to government for their policies and practices. What complicates matters is the necessary use of discretion. In their daily contact with the public, individual police officers use discretion in a number of ways. While their priority is the 'enforcement of the law', the law itself provides no hard-and-fast framework in which to operate. The law is ambiguous, open to interpretation, and occasionally contradictory. Police officers necessarily use their personal judgement to weigh up a situation and enforce the law. Laws that are framed ambiguously, such as the clause, 'action likely to cause a breach of the peace' in the 1936 Public Order Act, can in practice be used more extensively than was originally intended. Laws that are unambiguously framed, such as the Road Traffic Acts, are in practice used variably.

The decisions in these cases represent a variable mix of local force policy, often determined by the priorities of the chief constable, and the feelings or prejudices of individual officers. Abusive language may or may not lead to an arrest depending on its content and the circumstances (for example, kids on the street, strikers on a picket line, women at Greenham Common). All kinds of normally acceptable behaviour may be redefined as actions 'likely to cause a breach of the peace' if police officers so wish. This means that certain kinds of behaviour may be ignored or lead to a warning, an arrest, a caution or a charge. The course chosen by an officer in one situation does not necessarily provide any guide as to the course chosen in another situation. Similarly, different police officers react quite differently to the same situation. Having said that, there is considerable evidence, the most recent being the Policy Studies Institute Report on police-community relations commissioned by the Metropolitan Police,[1] to show that police responses are not always so arbitrary. The stereotyping of black people, working-class youth, strikers, the unemployed and other identifiable groups is strong in police culture, particularly in inner cities and large towns.

In the enforcement of the law police powers are extensive. Following the Royal Commission on Criminal Procedure, the two Thatcher administrations have drafted and, after opposition from a range of professional agencies, redrafted the Police and Criminal Evidence Act, 1984 (scheduled to become law in 1986). The new Act, more thoroughly discussed in Chapter 6, will further extend police powers. The police have the power to search and seize property providing that they have obtained a warrant signed by a magistrate. Warrants are rarely refused and because 'sympathetic' magistrates are known to the police they are often signed 'on the nod'. There exist no regulations governing the selection of or number of approaches made to magistrates by the police for warrants. The easy means through which warrants are obtained has come under considerable criticism, particularly after several raids were made 'in error' on the homes of old people by the West Midlands Police in 1982. Under the new Act the police will be able to apply for a warrant to search the houses of people not suspected of a crime if they have suspicion that there might be evidence there which relates to a serious arrestable offence.

Since the withdrawal of the controversial SUS laws, under which many people – particularly young blacks[2] – were arrested on the street for acting suspiciously, the police powers to 'stop and search' people have ostensibly been curtailed. If they can demonstrate reasonable suspicion that an offence has been committed, or is about to be committed, however, the police can stop people and search them and their vehicles or other possessions. There is considerable evidence that black people are still harassed by the police despite the withdrawal of SUS. On Merseyside, for example, stop and search is embodied in local bye-laws and has enabled harassment, so evident under SUS, to continue without effective challenge.[3] Under the new Act, stop and search will be extended to include 'equipment' for stealing. While this is covered by 'reasonable suspicion' the demonstration of 'reasonable' or 'suspicion' is difficult to contest after the event. Inevitably these interpretations come down to the word of the police officer/s against the word of the individual.

'Reasonable suspicion' is also at the centre of powers of arrest. A warrant is not necessary and the police can use 'reasonable force' to make an arrest. Section 3 of the 1967 Criminal Law Act states:

A person may use such force as is reasonable in the circumstances in the prevention of crime or in effecting or assisting in the lawful arrest of offenders or suspected offenders or of persons unlawfully at large.

These powers extend to all citizens and they formed the basis of the debate in the trial of two police officers in the Waldorf case. Their defence was that they believed that Waldorf was David Martin and, given that belief, they used an amount of force which would have been reasonable for the detention of Martin. Under the 1984 Act, the police will be given greater powers than those generally allowed to citizens. They will have the power to use force in stop and search on the street, to enter forcibly the houses of people not under suspicion of criminal activity, to take samples and fingerprints forcibly from people detained without charge and to use force in strip and intimate body searches.

Under the Act the police powers of arrest without a warrant are extended to include people suspected of committing any offence if they refuse to give their name or the name given is believed by the police to be false; if they have not given a 'satisfactory' address; if they might harm themselves or others, damage property, obstruct the highway or cause an 'affront to public decency'; if there is a child or other 'vulnerable' person at risk. An arrest will be lawful only if the person arrested is told that she or he is under arrest and the reason for the arrest. In some circumstances the police will have the automatic power to search the person and the place where the arrest took place.

Following an arrest, the police have powers to question, interrogate and detain a person. Under the Act, however, people can be detained without being charged with an offence for up to 24 hours on the authority of an inspector. The basis of this is to secure or preserve evidence or to enable questioning to continue. If a person is suspected of a 'serious arrestable offence' a superintendent can authorize a further extension for up to 96 hours' detention without charge. After a person has been charged she or he can be kept in detention if there is any doubt over the validity of name or address, if she or he might cause physical harm or loss/damage to property or, for juveniles, if it is in their 'best interest'. People charged should go before a magistrate's court at its next sitting.

'Serious arrestable offence' includes murder, rape, kidnapping, firearms and explosive offences, highjacking and hostage taking. It also includes *any* offence under the Prevention of Terrorism Act. The most controversial offences in this category, however, are those which *might* lead to serious harm to state security or public order, serious interference with the administration of justice, serious injury or death to another person, substantial gain or serious financial loss to anybody. This final category is clearly ambiguous because it is defined as 'having regard to all circumstances, serious for the person who suffers it'. Each of these categories reaffirms the broad operational discretion made available to police officers in defining 'seriousness' and thus being able to detain people without charge for up to four days.

A person under detention is protected nominally by the Judges' Rules and Administrative Directions to the Police (1912, revised: 1964) which are supposed to work as effective guidelines so that admissible evidence in court is of consistent quality. As the Rules are not statutory, they are not binding on police policies. In his evidence to the 1980 Royal Commission on Criminal Procedure, the Metropolitan Commissioner admitted that the Judges' Rules were habitually ignored by investigating officers. He defended this institutionalized malpractice by arguing that good and efficient police work was hindered by the Rules. Consequently he submitted that the Commission should recommend that police powers be *extended* to legitimate these well-established wrongful practices.

In effect, the 1984 Police Act responds to the Metropolitan Commissioner's demands. While a detainee will have the right to have a friend, relative or other person informed of her/his detention and the right to consult privately with a solicitor, *suspicion* of a 'serious arrestable offence' removes these rights. A superintendent can delay access for up to 36 hours or, for Prevention of Terrorism Act charges, for up to 48 hours. Searches for property, including strip searches, and intimate body searches (mouth, anus, vagina) are also permitted under the new Act. They can take place without consent and, if necessary, using force. Non-intimate body samples and fingerprints can be taken without consent on the authorization of a superintendent. 'Reasonable force' can be used.

Finally, the most significant of the powers possessed by the police is that of prosecution. In England and Wales only the most controversial or serious cases are handled by the Director of Public Prosecutions or the Attorney General. Consequently, the police selectively enforce the law, they detain and interrogate 'behind closed doors' and, finally, they construct the case for the prosecution. The procedure is geared to the establishing of guilt and the police prosecute if they consider that they have a reasonable chance of success. The DPP has stated that he proceeds with prosecution only when he thinks that he has a 'more than 50 per cent chance' of conviction. While this is probably the guiding principle for police prosecutions in serious cases which eventually will go before a jury, in taking minor cases to the magistrates' court they certainly do not limit themselves to a 50 per cent chance of conviction. Cases before magistrates are quite often based only on police evidence and there is a marked reluctance of magistrates to doubt police testimony. The most notorious example of this was the hearing of the cases which followed the 1979 Southall demonstration in which Blair Peach was killed by a police officer. The magistrates returned an unusually high conviction rate against mostly black people who had been prosecuted solely on the basis of police testimony. The Report of the Unofficial Committee of Inquiry[4] was in no doubt that most arrests and judgements were arbitrary. With this close connection between those who enforce the law, those who prosecute and those who make judgement, it is clear that police powers are extensive and rely heavily on discretion.

Police discretion, then, is developed at different levels, from the operational policies laid down by chief constables to the daily practices of officers on the beat. The police use discretion in their interpretation of the law and its application. They use discretion to determine the application of police force rules and their responses to the priorities of their senior command. Chief constables and their assistants use discretion in formulating policies and in their responses to their police authorities and the Home Secretary. This overall framework demonstrates the fundamental autonomy of the police.

Within the legal, organizational and political dimensions there exist few effective constraints on the exercise of discretion. Senior officers, such as Sir Robert Mark, remain rigid in their defence of the accountability of the police:

> The fact that the British police are answerable to the law,
> that we act on behalf of the community and not the mantle
> of government, makes us the least powerful, the most
> accountable and therefore the most acceptable police force
> in the world.[5]

Sir David McNee once commented that although the police have a unique responsibility for law enforcement, their position in relation to the law is the same as anyone else's. They are 'citizens in uniform'. Clearly the police are accountable to the law, but to say that their relationship is identical to that of others' is misleading. For it is the very form that the special relationship between the police and the law takes which places the police in a different position. Police work is specialized, professional and institutionalized. The police not only have to observe the law, they also enforce and apply it – and in that sense the law is in their keeping. Their lawful powers exceed anything possessed by other civilian institutions. While they have a primary duty to the law, the relationship, as we have seen, is not clear-cut or unambiguous. The new Police

Act will extend the powers of the police and legitimate their previous indiscretions.

The main procedure for making police officers accountable to the law is the complaints system. Complaints usually refer to specific acts of misconduct by police officers. They do not necessarily refer to law-breaking. Typical examples of such a complaint would be discourteous behaviour or rudeness. If found 'guilty', the officer concerned is reprimanded and the complainant receives a letter of apology. More serious complaints, such as alleged assault by an arresting officer would, if upheld, constitute law-breaking. The reports of the investigating officers are submitted to the Director of Public Prosecutions who then decides whether or not to prosecute. As we have seen, the DPP only prosecutes if it is considered that there is more than a half chance of conviction. As juries seem reluctant to convict police officers many genuine complaints never reach court. Furthermore, a fair number of complaints concern situations at which only the complainant and police officers were present. At the end of the day the main criticism of the complaints procedure is that it involves an internal investigation; the police policing the police. The complainant has no right of access to the investigator's report and in 1979 a High Court decision ruled such reports to be the property of the chief constable.

Accountability, according to successive contemporary commissioners, is a combination of the primacy of the law and the consent of the community. Sir David McNee recalled the directions of the first police commissioners, Rowan and Mayne, to emphasize the point: 'Their original instructions to the force made it clear that the old tradition of policing from within the community, with the consent of the community, was to be the guiding principle of the new system.'[6] The evidence in Chapter 2 denies that real community consent has ever been given to the police. What the police have come to define as the public's consent is a passive, grudging acceptance of a police presence. This consent has been traded in for police freedom from constitutional and political control. Senior officers thus reject the 'control' or 'political interference' of democratic government and its elected members. Consequently, the quite distinct categories of 'accountability' and 'control' are effectively merged.

A further formal check on police practices and conduct is provided by the internal disciplinary regulations of each police force. The disciplinary code is used at the discretion of senior officers to discipline and control subordinates and it provides an operational form of control additional to the law. The extent to which force discipline provides a check on the actions of police officers has to be considered within the framework of the occupational structure. Police forces are highly organized, professional institutions working, like other complex institutions, on the basis of informal as well as formal procedures. Career and management structures, specialized training and division of labour all contribute to hierarchical divisions and occupational splits. Senior officers initiate policy decisions and operational priorities for their force; the intermediate ranks establish the operational framework to carry them out; and the rank and file, under supervision and bound by internal regulations, put them into action. The Police Federation, the representative body of the rank and file, constantly criticizes senior officers for lack of consultation over operational policies and priorities.

The daily reality of police work, however, means that individual officers work long hours, sometimes in pairs, without any direct supervision. Most of their decisions demand an immediate, personal judgement. The police constable has considerable autonomy in defining and responding to specific situations. The only formal briefing which officers receive before handling difficult situations and different people is a woefully inadequate police training course. Consequently, the police receive most of their training on the job from other more experienced officers within the police work group. To some extent this occupational culture provides rank-and-file police officers with the basis to resist the objectives of 'managerial professionalism' – to deny the bosses their way. At the same time this informal training has the most powerful influence on police ideology. For it is in the confines of the messroom or the police club that the prejudices of the police appear most sharply. This is a camaraderie of survival, a uniting against the pressures of internal hierarchy and outside criticism; it is also a collective identity built on shared assumptions about race, gender, youth, class, unions, socialism, etc. It is within this occupational culture that the 'enemy' is defined, attitudes are shaped and prejudices reinforced. It was this issue, discussed fully in Chapter 5, which brought the most revealing and damning indictment of the Metropolitan Police by the Policy Studies Institute researchers.

The most controversial aspect of the debate on police autonomy concerns policy and priorities within and between the forces. As the police operate on a local basis, the powers possessed by chief constables for setting force priorities are considerable. There are central influences in the form of Home Office guidelines and directives, and there are regular visits from the Chief Inspector of Constabulary to promote levels of consistency. But how far, if at all, chief constables are constrained in their use of discretion is questionable. The central political constraint (the Home Secretary) and the local political constraint (the Police Authority) are embodied in the 1964 Police Act. The exception to this relationship is the Metropolitan Police whose police authority is the Home Secretary. Throughout the provincial forces the 1964 Act gave operational responsibility for policies and priorities to chief constables. They are expected to respond to advice offered to them by police authorities, whose membership is two-thirds elected councillors and one-third appointed magistrates. There is no obligation on chief constables to act on this advice nor do they have to justify their decisions in specific cases. They 'direct and control' the operations of their forces in consultation with their senior officers although such consultation is discretionary. Perhaps the most significant of their discussions are held with other chief constables; the Association of Chief Police Officers (ACPO) is highly influential in devising and carrying through 'common' policy decisions – an essential role in the 1984–5 coal dispute discussed in Chapter 7.

Chief constables have remained united and adamant on the question of political constraints. They have argued that any direct involvement (they prefer the term 'interference') by police authorities or politicians in the operational decisions of their forces would constitute a shift towards political control of the police. They portray this as a threat to police impartiality which would allow the police to be used in the interests of whichever political party happened to be in government. This is a difficult position to sustain, since senior officers also recognize that in the tradition of British police work they cannot be accountable *solely* to the law and still claim to be answerable to locally elected councillors on police committees. They argue this point by refusing direct political control and accepting *indirect public* accountability based on the notion of 'policing by consent'. It is the chief constables, however, who are the interpreters and definers of popular consent.

The loose, informal and self-assessed framework of 'indirect accountability' to the community has provided chief constables with a distinct operational and policy-making autonomy supported by successive home secretaries. The operational responsibility given to chief constables by the 1964 Police Act has helped to institutionalize police autonomy at the highest operational level. Chief constables can set priorities for law enforcement, target specific crimes or suspected individuals, saturate areas identified by the police as problem areas, instigate specialist squads, monitor identifiable groups, carry out surveillance on political and industrial activists and control the right to demonstrate. In all these cases, and there are many others, chief constables can claim that they are dealing with operational issues and so deny information to elected representatives. In this way successive Metropolitan Commissioners have been able to instruct the Special Patrol Group to swamp areas with a high concentration of black residents, against the explicit wishes of local authorities. It is this denial of democracy, which Mark, McNee and Newman have all been so eager to preserve, which has raised most concern over police autonomy. For the police cannot remain outside the usual checks and balances of political responsibility, accountable to neither local nor national government, and still claim to be 'democratic'.

It is perhaps not surprising that the police should want to operate unfettered by political affiliation on a similar basis to the so-called independence of the judiciary. To some extent judges accept the primacy of the legislature in the matter of who makes the laws. The police, however, contest the supremacy of elected representatives in establishing police priorities. Mark's position favours consent when *informally* expressed, but not when *formally* expressed through the democratic process. The notion of consent here is both narrow and nebulous.

The triangle of political accountability

The role of the Home Secretary is typical of the lack of clarity in the relationship between government and police. The Home Secretary is supposed to maintain a watching brief on police policies and practices as well as being the police authority for the metropolitan area. At first glance it would seem that this dual function places him in an influential, if not controlling, position. He might be expected to play a significant part in the development of strategies in the capital and also to be in regular consultation, issuing directives when and where appropriate, with provincial chief constables and police authorities. How far the Home Secretary effectively influences the Metropolitan Commissioner, or any other chief constable, remains unclear. Answers to parliamentary questions asked by MPs give a very inadequate picture of the Home Secretary's role: a survey of parliamentary questions asked about the Metropolitan Police revealed that *one-sixth* were refused even a reply.[7] There is no clear indication of how frequent his interventions are or what form they take. However, it is clear that successive Home Secretaries have been reluctant either to intervene in matters of policy or to criticize chief constables for their handling of particular events.

In 1961, following a series of 'spectacular' cases of police misconduct and malpractice, a Royal Commission on the Police was set up. There was already considerable concern that organized crime was out of control and that the police were becoming directly involved in its development. There was also disquiet over the handling of the CND demonstrations, prosecutions of officers for planting evidence, the beating of arrested strikers at the Roberts-Arundel strike and the prosecution of two chief constables. On all fronts – crime, public order and industrial conflict – there were serious doubts about the abuse of powers by the police and the effectiveness of controls.

The 1929 Royal Commission on Police Powers and Procedure had stated that a chief constable 'is responsible to his authority which is a unit of local government'. The 1962 Royal Commission, however, gave a very different account:

He is accountable to no-one and subject to no-one's orders for the way in which, for example, he settles his general policies in regard to law enforcement over the area covered by his force, the concentration of his resources on any particular type of crime or area, the manner in which he handles political demonstrations or processions and allocates and instructs his men when preventing breaches of the peace arising from industrial disputes, the methods he employs in dealing with an outbreak of violence or of passive resistance to authority, his policy in enforcing the traffic laws and dealing with parked cars, and so on.

The Royal Commission rejected the idea of a 'national' police force and recommended the amalgamation of forces. It went on to say that 'the problem of controlling the police can therefore be restated as the problem of controlling chief constables'. What was needed was 'more effective supervision' of chief constables – though no compromising of their 'impartiality in enforcing the law in particular cases'. The Association of Municipal Authorities wanted to be given effective means of making the police more accountable but the police organizations said they would not accept such control. The Royal Commission attempted to steer a middle course and recommended that chief constables 'should be free from the conventional process of democratic control and influence', should 'enjoy immunity from orders' but still be 'made responsible' to the newly formed police authorities. These should give 'advice and guidance' to chief officers who 'would be expected to take heed'. If this advice and guidance was continually ignored, then the chief constable's 'fitness for office' would be under review. In order to maintain a watching brief on chief constables, both the police authorities and the Home Secretary could request reports, additional to the chief constable's annual report, on specific events. Chief constables, however, would not be obliged to provide such reports. In practice, reports are rarely refused but their content and thoroughness is dictated by chief constables' discretion.

The problem of the political accountability of the police was compounded by the Royal Commission. It was recognized that police officers possessed 'original authority' and not 'delegated authority' in so far as their primary duty was to the rule of law and not to political rule. However, it was also recognized that chief officers should be accountable to the representatives of the electorate. Against the stated intention of greater local controls on the police, it was asserted that the police 'ought to be impartial and uninfluenced by external pressures'. The Association of Municipal Authorities' campaign for 'executive control' of the police – which did not include any right of police authorities to become involved in specific cases – was lost in the Commission's compromise. What the Commission attempted was to balance police 'impartiality' with a 'degree of supervision'. Thus the new police authorities (commonly known as police committees), two-thirds councillors and one-third magistrates, were set up; the Home Secretary's supervisory role was developed and the forces eventually expanded through amalgamation.

The Association of Municipal Authorities continued its opposition: it was unhappy with the extension of the Home Secretary's supervisory role, with the concept of original authority, with the strengthening of chief constables' powers over operational policy, with the diminution of police committee powers and with the appointment of magistrates to police authorities. This concern, along with an acceptance that police powers and the democratic control of the police were ill-defined, was recognized by the Royal Commission.

All of these ambiguities and contradictions were reflected in the 1964 Police Act. The primary function of police authorities was defined as being 'to secure the maintenance of an adequate and efficient police force for their area', while the operation of the force was firmly placed under the 'direction and control of the chief constable'. Police authorities were appointed to hire and fire chief constables (subject to the Home Secretary's approval), to determine the rank hierarchy, to maintain the force establishment, to provide and maintain adequate buildings, vehicles and equipment and to approve the budget, the latter being a significant form of control. They were also given responsibility for senior officers' discipline and for overseeing 'the manner in which complaints are dealt with'. This did not mean that police authorities were to be involved in specific cases or individual complaints. While the Royal Commission stated quite precisely that chief constables needed closer control and supervision, its recommendations, reflected in the secondary status of the police authority given by the Act, gave the *appearance* of greater accountability, but *in reality* guaranteed the relative autonomy of chief constables.

One of the most significant terms of reference of the Royal Commission on the Police was to examine 'the status and accountability of members of police forces, including chief officers of police'. The Commission's Report and the Police Act which followed had major implications for police powers at a senior level. While the idea of a national force was rejected, the powers of chief officers were extended by the encouragement of amalgamation. In 1962 there were 152 forces in Great Britain, of which 125 were in England and Wales. As a result of the policy of amalgamation in the sixties and the reorganization of local government in the seventies, there are, in 1985, only 51 forces in Great Britain of which 43 are in England and Wales. Undoubtedly this has increased the powers of individual chief officers. Some senior officers have argued for a still further reduction – to about ten forces – while others have called for a national police force.

According to T.A. Critchley, the change to fewer and larger forces has increased the 'status of the chief constable' and 'provided the opportunity for greater cohesion between chief constables in policy making'.[8] He also argues that force amalgamations and local authority reorganization has dismembered many of the old police authorities and thus that the understanding and experience of well-established members has been lost. The new authorities were inexperienced and had no 'familiarity with local police operations'. His comment on the redesignated West Midlands, with its seven metropolitan districts and its central police authority, is instructive:

> It is already clear that some of the newly constituted police authorities are anxious to play a more positive part in police affairs. They find the curbs set to their powers by the Police Act 1964 irksome, and hanker after a readjustment of their relationship with the chief constable so as to *redress the balance in favour of greater responsibility and democratic control*.[9] (Emphasis added)

This echoes the sentiments of police committees at the time of the Royal Commission and of the evidence submitted by the Association of Municipal Authorities. Other studies argued that by the mid-1970s the procedures for consultation and accountability had become outmoded and inappropriate. Michael Banton, for example, felt that the police were less accountable in the larger areas particularly as police authority members had little 'personal acquaintance and shared understanding' of the communities they served.[10] He considered that the selective enforcement of the law, the allocation of scarce resources and an independent assessment of the wishes of the public should be 'checked against the views of members of the police committee'. His final criticism was that on a range of issues the framework of police authorities was not responsive to developments in criminal activity and the subsequent police response. He suggested a much wider framework of consultation involving other state agencies and a much greater interventionist role by police committees on general policy matters. The Police Federation and ACPO responded that the police should not be singled out from other state institutions for special scrutiny. They were opposed to the involvement of 'outsiders' in the policy-making process and in police responses to specific situations.

A strong attack on police authorities was made by Margaret Simey in 1976. She argued that police committees operated 'with the brake permanently on' and this she blamed on the 'calculatedly non-political and non-accountable' magistrate members. Again the focus of her criticism was the 1964 Police Act, 'which in effect set police authorities free from the direct political accountability required of other local government committees'. The police committees' work was not questioned or scrutinized to the same extent as other local authority committees and there was a tacit acceptance that 'there is no political context in the work of the police committee'. She concluded:

> The be-all and end-all of a police committee is therefore
> assumed to be the exercise of what must of necessity be no
> more than the remotest of control over police activity . . .
> Police committees are reduced to being not very effective
> cogs in the administrative system of a public service.
> Committee agendas consist entirely of items relating to the
> efficiency and adequacy of the staff. The force, the whole
> force, and nothing but the force is the sole subject of our
> discussions.[11]

Thus it was Margaret Simey's opinion that the police committees' lack of involvement in operational policies, priorities and practices, together with the reluctance of the local council to oversee the work of police committees, provided the police with independence from the community. She claimed that the price of taking politics out of police work was the loss of democratic control. Her solution was to argue for the development of political purpose in which police work would become a responsibility shared by police authorities, as community representatives, and chief constables.

In response to Margaret Simey's article, the editor of *Police* magazine, Tony Judge, argued that police authorities were 'beyond resuscitation'.[12] He maintained that chief constables and the Home Office were 'united in their determination not to increase the role of the police committee'. Once again, the main thrust of the police position turned on the issue of political intervention. He argued that shared responsibility was not feasible without a direct political challenge to the operational authority of chief constables. He was in no doubt that the real power lay in the hands of chief constables and that any police committee which took on a chief constable 'would soon find itself reminded of its responsibility for efficiency'. These sentiments had been stated clearly in a joint conference of ACPO and local authorities in 1975. In a paper published later in *Police Review* it was stressed that police authorities 'must stop short of seeking to interfere with the day-to-day running, the operational responsibilities of the chief constable'.[13] It stated that while police authorities should provide a 'lively forum' for discussion, their function was solely advisory. It endorsed Judge's position and emphasized the special powers and authority of chief constables.

If this position ever needed support it was to be found in the judiciary. In 1968, for example, Lord Denning had ruled that a chief constable

is not a servant of anyone save the law itself. No Minister of the Crown can tell him that he must, or must not, keep observation on this place or that; or that he must, or must not, prosecute this man or that one. Nor can any police authority tell him so. The responsibility for law enforcement lies on him. He is answerable to the law and the law alone.[14]

4. Misadventure on Merseyside

This chapter provides a unique case history of conflict between a police committee and its chief constable. In 1979 serious criticisms were directed at the Chief Constable of Merseyside, Kenneth Oxford, concerning allegations of police brutality in the K Division area of the Merseyside Police Force. With the death in police custody of Jimmy Kelly and eyewitness accounts alleging that he was assaulted on arrest, K Division became the subject of national media coverage. The minority Labour group on the Police Committee demanded an explanation of the affair from the Chief Constable. His angry response indicated that the Police Committee had no right to interfere in matters of operational policy and practice. Within a short time the events on Merseyside became the first real test of the effectiveness of the political powers of police authorities as laid down in the 1964 Police Act.

While the row over K Division continued, two further significant events occurred on Merseyside. In 1981 the Labour Party gained a clear majority on the Metropolitan Council and thus became the dominant group on the Police Committee. At the same time trouble flared in many cities and towns as black communities, supported by many working-class whites, took to the streets in anti-police uprisings. Toxteth, in the heart of Liverpool, became a battleground throughout the summer months. The police operation was massive and the cost, in injuries and money, unprecedented. For months police officers throughout Britain were deployed in Merseyside neighbourhoods. The hard-line policies and practices of the Merseyside police, which had been endured for over a decade by Liverpool blacks, were criticized forcefully, as was Oxford's use of CS gas and other offensive tactics to put down the Toxteth uprising.

This chapter examines these events within the context of the structure of police powers and accountability. It uses the confrontations between the Police Committee and the Chief Constable in 1979–82 as a means of evaluating the real, as opposed to theoretical, powers available to police authorities. Thus it questions the basis of the political accountability of the police.

The first section considers the argument that police authorities neglect to use the powers available to them. The second section traces the controversy which arose out of the events in Knowsley, Merseyside, during the summer of 1979. The third section examines the Toxteth uprising, the police response and the subsequent conflict between the Chief Constable and the Police Committee. The final section critically assesses the role and actual powers of both the Chief Constable and the Police Committee in the light of the Merseyside confrontation.

A voluntary misuse of responsibility?

In 1980, just as the Merseyside confrontation over the power of the Police Committee was at its height, Martin Kettle wrote a short article on the workings of police committees.[1] It focused on the Thames Valley Police which covers the authorities of Oxfordshire, Berkshire and Buckinghamshire and is a product of the amalgamations of smaller forces. The police committee is composed of elected councillors from the three councils and the statutory one-third appointed magistrates. In 1980 the Chairman was a magistrate member and there were only three non-Tory councillors on the committee. The Chairman commented, 'the authority is virtually non-political'. Given the class background of most magistrates and the curious, anachronistic and secret system of patronage which underlies JP appointments, the police authority was dominated by Tory politics. At one of the meetings Kettle attended the Chief Constable argued for an increased establishment estimated to cost £7.5 million. Being a financial matter, and one which clearly fell within the statutory role of the police authority to maintain an adequate and efficient force, the committee was centrally involved in the decision over the extra budget. The meeting agreed to the Chief Constable's demand. Kettle concluded:

> The members were obviously quite happy with the decision and the way it was reached . . . Perhaps you wouldn't expect such a predominantly conservative part of the country to

cavil at new levels. But whether by design or accident, the meeting ended up by granting wide discretionary powers to the Chairman and Chief Constable over an item involving a possible 16 per cent rise in expenditure and with wide policing implications. What's more, the item wasn't even on the agenda for the authority meeting. It is hard to avoid concluding that most members neither know nor care much about controlling what is happening.

Kettle called this the 'voluntary misuse of responsibility' which results in important information – such as the extent and type of arms held by the force – not being available to the public. Thus the information which comes from the police is that which the chief constable sees fit to release. According to Kettle there is no way of resolving conflicts between a police authority and a chief constable 'except in the chief constable's favour'. He concluded that 'any local moves to impose a new model of policing in opposition to the police will soon find out the severe limits of the existing local accountability system, as the reality of national co-ordination of policing asserts itself'.

The 'misuse of responsibility' by police authority members has created a style of political operation which has come to dominate the question of accountability. The police position is to merge the categories of control and accountability. Political intervention in operational and policy matters is rejected – the police must resist what they see as political control. During the mid-1970s Michael Banton raised the issue of effective participation on police committees.[2] In reply to a question about consulting the police committee over the redeployment of officers, a chief constable of an amalgamated police force stated plainly that he would not even consider such consultation. Answering a question on the powers of police authorities to call for reports under the 1964 Police Act, he stated, 'I don't think any member of my police authority has read the Act and I hope none of them does.' What emerged from Banton's discussions, however, was that 'any change in the membership of police committees introduces a question which will evoke passionate responses in police quarters'. He concluded:

Many policemen at present are bitterly critical of the supposed influence of local politicians upon police affairs.

'It's farcical that a group of plumbers and butchers can dictate to the Chief Constable,' said one. 'What does an accountant know about police problems?' 'One of them asked me if a chief inspector was higher than a chief superintendent!' said another.

The consistent theme here is the protection by the police of their autonomy in all areas of their work. It is this which leads to compliance, if not deference, on the part of police authorities.

The only research of any depth into the workings of police committees was conducted on Merseyside by Mike Brogden in 1977.[3] It is worth reproducing a selection of the quotes from interviews with committee members:

'The Chief Constable never needs to justify his resources . . . all the figures are there . . . we're all laymen. We can't quarrel with the figures.' (Councillor)

'Frankly, I've never understood what our powers were . . . this was one of the earliest questions that I asked. It seemed rather a waste of time going to a committee where one has no powers of any kind, particularly when you're a senior chap in the law as I am, and I quite frankly don't know what our powers are at all, and I don't think that we do fulfil any great purpose.' (Magistrate member)

'What do we talk about? – the sick, the lame and the lazy . . . There's nothing meaty about the agenda at all – medical matters, awards to police officers, the closure of police stations, the annual inspections – we never discuss the actual operations of the police.' (Alderman)

'The basic function of the police authority is the pensioning off of old officers and the like – we are never more than on the fringe of any activity of the police . . . I regard this committee as a complete waste of time. I stay on it as a public-spirited sort of chap – some magistrates did resign . . . because we were completely ineffective. (Magistrate member)

Brogden's research concluded that the Police Committee was 'inundated with data of a largely insignificant nature' which presented 'an image of the force as a painstaking body of experts'. With financial matters minimized and the issues in question apparently covered in depth, the committee was more often than not presented with a *fait accompli* against which members were ill equipped to argue: 'The Chief Constable's office effectively controls the issues under discussion and preempts the decision-making process.' According to the majority of committee members interviewed, the Police Committee was devoid of political debate and the questioning of officers associated with local authority committees. They felt that it was little more than 'a "rubber stamp" for the wishes of the Chief Constable'.

Paul Okojie and Maria Noble conducted a study in 1980 of northern police authorities, one of them Merseyside. Its findings reinforce the range of issues covered by the earlier studies and gives some insight into the selection of police authority members. Selection of elected members to the police committee is seen as a 'reward for seniority in a party's pecking order' and the process is 'based on an "informal code" designed to maintain the "consensus" character of police authorities'. Selection of magistrate members, carried out by the Magistrates Courts Committee, is also based on seniority, indeed it is common for the Chairman of the Bench to sit on the police authority.

Thus the police committee has rarely been an arena for political controversy. Decisions concerning the agenda, the content and future policies appear to be settled prior to meetings. The committee maintains an unquestioning consensus which virtually guarantees a chief constable direct rule over the decision-making process. Okojie and Noble show that the police committee is more likely to debate the cost of dog biscuits than to discuss the priorities for police intervention.

Knowsley: the summer of 1979

If you pick up James McLure's *Spike Island: A Portrait of a Police Division*,[5] you cannot help feeling that you have entered a war zone. Researched and written in the late 1970s, the book focuses on the policing of inner-city Liverpool immediately before the Toxteth uprising. According to the Merseyside Chief Constable, it 'faithfully portrays the frequently hectic, often dangerous task' which faces the police where 'crime and disorder are ever-present and have always been so throughout the turbulent history of the city'.[6] McLure bolsters this impression by claiming that a major characteristic of Liverpudlians is 'an astonishing propensity for gratuitous violence', an 'evil streak' which produces 'dreadful injuries far in excess of any need'. He quotes extensively from a 'softly spoken' veteran police officer who describes how a 'new bobby' is introduced to the division:

> To his left, the North Sub [sub-division], and it's a bit of a desert island that side. All those cliff-dwellers in high-rise flats; the bucks running wild and a few buckesses too . . . then straight in front of him, the market place: all that glitters, merchants and moneylenders, beggars and meths-drinkers lying about legless! . . . Then, to his right, the South Sub [sub-division]: the jungle noises and even more the jungle behaviour of clubland; then yellow people country, Chinatown; then, up in the right-hand top corner, black people country, Upper Parliament Street, a bit of Liverpool 8 . . . Then, if he's coming on Nights, he'll probably see five sort of stockades with campfires burning; places he can get in out of the cold and be safe from a hiding for a while . . .

This is the place 'said to have the country's worst law and order problem'. The juxtaposition of assertions about apparently genetic, or at least culturally learned, violent characteristics of 'Liverpudlians' and the emphasis on territory in such descriptions as 'jungle' land, 'black people country' and so on gives the impression that violence and a conscious disregard for *all* law is inevitable. If you're not born bad, you'll soon catch it. No one escapes this inner-city web of violence, except the consensual, white, semidetached middle classes, to whom this lawlessness is a persistent threat. It justifies hard-line policing – a tough, rough people need a tough, rough police force. Hence the 'war zone' – 'them' and 'us' – a situation in which the imagery is not only reflected in the attitudes and practices of police officers on the streets but one where it is deeply institutionalized in operational policy at the most senior levels.

The conflict between inner-city communities and the Merseyside

Police over police responses to working-class practices, industrial conflict and political demonstrations has a long history. In the late 1960s and 1970s it became apparent that discriminatory policing and racist abuse against Liverpool's black population would lead to major confrontations similar to those of the 1930s. The uneasy peace was interspersed with occasional confrontations over the failure to deal with white racism, the planting of drugs, arrest on suspicion, stop and search and alleged brutality. The apparent institutionalization of these practices added to the growing concern over police racism. Thus a police force already geared to hard-line methods in the inner city during the early seventies showed a strong hostility towards the black community. As in other cities, the black community wanted a police presence but one which provided protection against white racism. The seventies was a decade of mounting resistance and to all of us who lived in the inner city it was only a matter of time before there would be a full-scale confrontation. What no one had foreseen, however, was that the first crisis over police methods and accountability would break elsewhere in Merseyside: the district of Knowsley.

Knowsley is a long busride from the city centre. It is one of the five Metropolitan District Councils which constitute Merseyside and it contains two quite different post-war developments: the Huyton Industrial Estate and Kirkby New Town. With nearly 79,000 jobs lost in Merseyside in the 1970s and official unemployment running at 13 per cent throughout the Merseyside Special Development Area by 1979, these communities of 1960s expansion bore the brunt. Kirkby has long had a reputation for high levels of unemployment, poor housing and high incidence of crime. It also has one of the youngest populations in western Europe and recently the 'bulge' in the age distribution has been apparent in the school-leaving figures. On the Knowsley estates almost all the recent school leavers tread the well-worn path to the dole office. It is difficult to find a family untouched by unemployment. Yet these were the communities built on the promise of better housing, secure jobs and good living standards. Within one generation those expectations have diminished to the level of short-term government-backed training programmes. These schemes are nothing but cosmetic on estates such as those in Knowsley and their use of cheap, easily disposable and unprotected labour is deeply resented.

The resentment of those who have been made redundant is

sharpened by the realization that many will probably never work again on a permanent basis. It is inevitable and understandable that a whole range of small-scale criminal or underground-economy activities – welfare and unemployment 'fraud', moonlighting, petty crime, street gambling and selling 'off the back of a lorry' – have become an essential part of the local economy. These activities are well established and well known to the police. The pubs, for example, which serve as the marketplace for buying and selling, are known throughout the city. Just as the communities have grudgingly accepted the police, so the police have tolerated the activities of street economies. This well-established climate of mutual recognition and tolerance changed suddenly during the summer of 1979.

A member of the Jimmy Kelly Action Committee, set up in the wake of a series of sudden police interventions summed it up as follows,

> People used to know where they stood – how far they could go . . . I don't just mean in knocking off but in havin' a joke with the bobbies an' that . . . but after the bust-up at the Huyton Park you daren't say a word to them . . . just put your head down an' keep walking.[7]

What happened at the Huyton Park Hotel on 15 June 1979 was officially described as an 'organized police operation . . . to detect licensing offences'. Local people, on the other hand, believed it to be reprisal for damage done to a police car a week earlier. A number of people were arrested at the hotel for assaulting police officers or for being drunk and disorderly. Among these were three people who claimed that they had been assaulted by the police. In court it was alleged that officers gave perjured evidence. Two of these defendants were acquitted. Fourteen people lodged complaints against the police concerning assault during the arrests or perjury in the court. None of these complaints led to any disciplinary action. The evening after the Huyton Park Hotel incident another confrontation broke out in Huyton at the 'Eagle and Child' public house. Two officers were injured and five men arrested, one of whom, called Peter Jeonney, was sentenced to three years' imprisonment for affray and assault. The convictions were subsequently quashed following an Appeal Court ruling that the police evidence was inconsistent and therefore unsafe.

Matters came to a tragic end when on 21 June a Huyton man, Jimmy Kelly, was arrested for being drunk and disorderly on his way home from the 'Oak Tree' public house. Eyewitnesses claimed that police officers beat him severely and later threw him, handcuffed onto the floor of a police minibus. Jimmy Kelly died soon after in police custody. His injuries were extensive, including a fractured jaw, and in the opinion of a pathologist, Dr John Torry, were consistent with a severe beating.[8] The death of Jimmy Kelly became the catalyst for the organization of resistance in the local community. The Jimmy Kelly Action Committee was founded and extended its work to include a demand for a full inquiry into all of the incidents in K Division during the summer of 1979.

On 2 August a disturbance between neighbours occurred in Prescot. The police went to the Yates family house and arrested Mr and Mrs Yates and their son, Steven. Eyewitnesses said that Steven was kicked, kneed and punched by the police; his father was kicked while he lay motionless on the ground; and his mother was kicked as she ran to their aid. After a very painful night in police custody Betty Yates went to hospital where her injuries kept her for four days. All three were charged with assault occasioning actual bodily harm, criminal damage, and obstructing the police. These charges were eventually dropped, without any full explanation.

Three weeks after Yates family arrest, the police broke up a street dice game in Kirkby. One of the players, 18-year-old Michael Cavanagh ran away. He stated that when the police caught him he was kicked in the side and spent three hours at the police station, in pain and with no medical aid, before being released. Later he was rushed into hospital; he had fractured ribs and a five-hour operation failed to save his kidney and spleen. There followed a formal complaint from his family that he had been the victim of serious assault by the police and that they had failed to provide proper medical attention while in police custody. The complaint was not upheld.

In a series of articles published in the *New Statesman* Rob Rohrer argued that these incidents had produced a 'major breakdown in public confidence' with public 'allegations of extreme brutality made against the police'. His articles disclosed a crisis not simply over specific cases, although they were serious in themselves, but over operational policy and police accountability.

Local people, their local councillors and their MP Sir Harold

Wilson wanted to know why there had been an apparent move to hard-line, aggressive policing during this ten-week period. Was it part of a specific campaign or clampdown in Knowsley? Had directives come from 'the top' or were they part of local division initiatives? Were they simply the product of over-zealous local officers? Had the Police Committee been consulted? It was to the Merseyside Police Committee that people turned. Margaret Simey, a councillor member who led the Labour group on the Committee, responded:

> We are simply rubber stamps. We have the right to ask for
> information, the Chief Constable has the right to refuse. We
> should be having a discussion with the Chief Constable
> about the reasons the public are agin the police . . . The
> answer is a political one. It is not a police one. And the
> Chief Constable is in a right political pickle over Knowsley.

Harold Wilson called for a public inquiry into the death in custody of Jimmy Kelly. The Knowsley District Council responded to the Chief Constable with a no-confidence vote in the policing of their district. The media carried major features on the cases including serious allegations from eyewitnesses. The main points at issue now were the accountability of the police and the operational autonomy of the Chief Constable.

In the course of a BBC 'Panorama' special investigation Margaret Simey enlarged her attack on the police:

> I'm disturbed because the police have taken over the whole
> field of political decision, and police committees generally
> have opted out of their responsibility. The new chief
> constables are not PC Plod at all. They are very intelligent,
> very efficient people; but perhaps for that very reason
> unwilling to share their powers with elected representatives.[9]

The Merseyside Chief Constable, Kenneth Oxford, complained to the BBC that their 'inquiries were both impertinent and presumptuous'.[9] He accused Merseyside councillors, including some on the police committee, of 'vituperative and misinformed comment',[10] and claimed that the responsibility for a 'one-sided trial' of his force lay with 'certain sections of the media' and with 'others of dubious political intent'. The Chairman of the Police Federation at the time, James Jardine, claimed the critics of the Merseyside Police were 'the usual ragbag of people who spend their time sniping at the police service.'[11]

At a Police Committee meeting the Chief Constable was asked to give further details of the inquiry into the death of Jimmy Kelly. Members were told that he had nothing to add to his press statement which had preceded the meeting. Margaret Simey commented after the meeting that 'if we are talking about accountability and democracy then they should co-operate with the local Police Committee . . . We are now just reduced to "okaying" administrative items.'[12]

As the internal investigation dragged on into 1980, under the direction of an Assistant Chief Constable from the West Midlands Force, David Gerty, criticisms of the Merseyside Chief Constable came from the leaders of both the Tory and the Labour groups on the Merseyside Council. Sir Kenneth Thompson, then Chairman of the Metropolitan Council, attacked Oxford: 'At times he's arrogant . . . he talks of *his* police force. It isn't . . . it's *our* police force.'[13] He went on to mount a general attack on the 'distant authoritarianism of certain ego-inflated chief police officers' as a 'small group of intriguers who shape public opinion'. Councillor John Hamilton, Leader of the Labour Group on the Metropolitan Council, stated that 'the Chief Constable has indicated that the police force is quite separate from the County Council and the Police Committee'.[14] Hamilton argued that the Merseyside confrontation was 'symptomatic of a number of chief constables who are talking in this vein'. He concluded that 'the powers of the police authorities are nearly nonexistent at the present moment'.

In his Annual Report for 1979, the Chief Constable answered his critics thus:

> The tragic Kelly case was further cited to illustrate my
> reluctance to inform my police authority of matters
> pertinent to their responsibility: again completely
> unfounded and untrue, but unfortunately seized upon by
> those who question the accountability of chief police
> officers.

He stated that the Kelly case had given rise to 'grave calumnies' on the British police service and chief officers, but he gave no clarification as to the identity of 'those who question'.

In 1980, following the row between the Police Committee and Oxford, the Committee published a report by the County Solicitor which reinforced the well-established deference of police authorities to the operational decisions of the police:

> We recognize, however, whilst it is our duty to ensure that the policing of the area is both adequate and efficient we must at all times have regard for the need not to appear to be intervening in the statutory processes which the police must follow in carrying out their duties. As to how effectively the Police Committee carries out its duties must inevitably depend in the final analysis on the manner in which each and every member approaches the task.[15]

Thus the effectiveness of the committee was reduced to individual judgement and the basis of that judgement hinged on 'appearances' rather than realities. No efficient and thorough structure of accountability could be built on such shifting foundations. The Home Secretary rejected the case for a public inquiry into Jimmy Kelly's death which the Council had continued to press for. The Director of Public Prosecutions decided that the evidence submitted to him by the police investigation was insufficient to prosecute any of the officers involved with the case. The report on all the K Division cases was never made public.

Nine months after his death and following examination by three pathologists, the inquest into the death of Jimmy Kelly was held. The verdict was death by misadventure. Kenneth Oxford stated that this verdict 'cleared the individual officers involved and the Merseyside Police from the many allegations and criticisms which were made after this incident occurred which have now been found to be without substance'.[16] The Chief Constable issued a stone-walling report to the Police Committee in September 1980 on the conduct of K Division.

> The conclusions in each case so far resolved have revealed no grounds for police officers to be prosecuted in criminal courts or to be the subject of discipline procedures in accordance with police regulations . . . (Para.7)

> There is little doubt that the more obdurate critics will continue to denigrate the police, as is their wont, and will attempt to transform individual transgressions by police officers into a universal condemnation of the police system . . . (Para. 18)

The results of the internal investigations into K Division and the subsequent 'independent' police investigation were the exclusive property of the Chief Constable. Neither the Police Committee nor a coroner was empowered to order the publication of these reports. The extent of the Chief Constable's reply to requests for information on specific cases or general policy matters was shown to be entirely at his discretion. Despite all the eyewitness accounts, media coverage, political pressure, statements of concern and unanswered questions, the Chief Constable's brief reply on the Knowsley cases was the last word in the accountability debate.

Toxteth: the summer of 1981

In July and August 1981 many cities and towns in England and Wales experienced the most serious civil disturbances in the postwar period. They followed major confrontations between the police and the black community on the streets of St Paul's, Bristol in April 1980 and Brixton in April 1981. Amid the confused outrage enflamed by a near-hysterical popular press and by wild, opportunist statements from Tory politicians, the daily reality of the military oppression in the north of Ireland paled into insignificance. For the summer disturbances – commonly identified as 'The Riots' – were *really* serious: they were on *home* ground. It was no longer the 'safe distance' of Derry or Belfast, but the very heart of '*our* cities'. By any standards what happened on Merseyside was of major significance to understanding police-community relations and to the issue of 'policing by consent'.

Between 6 July and 15 August, 781 police officers were injured.[17] Of these just under 10 per cent were detained in hospital. Two-thirds of the overall injured came from the Merseyside Police force. 'Mutual aid' came from 40 other police forces which included 690 police support units. Each unit had one inspector, three sergeants and 30 constables. The cost of the police operation was enormous. Merseyside paid only for overtime, travelling and other associated costs of the officers sent from other forces. This came to £1,165,000. The estimated costs of Merseyside's own overtime and rest-day bill came to just under £3 million. Other items included: food and refreshment, £146,000; buses, carriers, telephone links, etc., £25,000; protective helmets, riot shields and other (non-specified) equipment, £56,000; protective work on existing vehicles, £30,000; security at stations, £6,000. The total bill was just under £4½ million, of which £2½ million was received from the Home Office in the form of a 60 per cent grant. The Chief Constable estimated that a further £364,000 would need to be spent on the re-equipment of '3,000 men with riot equipment', vehicles, station security and special rioting training. In terms of 'operational costs from 16 August, 1981' the Chief Constable stated: 'there is a continuing need for extra policing and it is anticipated that to the 31 August 1981, an additional £1 million will be required and, thereafter, £9,800 per day.'[18] Clearly these costs were substantial and, given the Police Committee's statutory responsibility for finance, an issue of public concern. The Chief Constable, as we shall see, ran into difficulty over his unauthorized expenditure of £56,000 on riot equipment.

Other police estimates included £500,000 worth of property stolen and just under £3½ million damaged. There were 1,070 recorded crimes, of which just over half were for wounding, and there were 320 arrests for offences in Toxteth. Between 9 and 12 July there were 'sporadic outbreaks of disorder' throughout Merseyside and 311 people were arrested in places other than Toxteth. A total of 214 police vehicles were damaged and there were 88 complaints against the police. It is impossible to estimate the number of civilians injured during the disturbances as many who were injured, some quite seriously, would not go for hospital treatment for fear of being implicated in the disturbances. One man, David Moore, who was physically disabled, was run down and killed by a police van driven along a footpath. He had not been in any way involved in the disturbances. Another man, Paul Conroy, suffered severe back injuries after being hit by a police land rover driven into a crowd. Photographs show the police dragging Conroy by his arms into a waiting police van.

For the first time in mainland Britain CS gas was fired by the police. This happened during the early hours of 6 July. The police used 18 rounds of 1½-inch canisters, seven rounds of 1½-inch

Ferret cartridges, 34 rounds of 12-bore Ferret cartridges and 15 grenades. As a result of the use of 41 Ferret cartridges, designed to be used on buildings or in a 'barrier-penetrating role' and clearly marked as such, four civilians were seriously injured.

How far could the magnitude of the events in Toxteth have been anticipated? Oxford is quoted as saying, 'I don't think anyone made any preparation for this lot'.[19] Only weeks before the disturbances he published his annual report in which he said that police-community relations in Toxteth were 'in a very healthy position and I do not foresee any difficulties in the future'. These statements are in direct contradiction to all independent research on and community accounts of the police presence in Toxteth throughout the 1960s and 1970s. Indiscriminate arrests, arbitrary stops and searches, physical and verbal aggression, racist abuse and the institutionalization of harassment have constituted the receiving end of police practice in the community. As Margaret Simey remarked in 1971,

> The black community is fed up of being hounded. No-one is
> safe on the streets after 10 p.m. One gang we know has
> given the police an ultimatum to lay off within two weeks or
> they fight back. It could lead to civil war in the city.

With rival youth-club fights portrayed as 'race riots', 'barricades' on the streets and rumours of petrol bombs given credibility, it appeared to the hysterical media that Powell's 'rivers of blood' were about to run in the streets of Toxteth. The constant pressure of 'meat wagons' – long, wheel-based, reinforced police land rovers – on the nightly tours of Toxteth made it abundantly clear that the police considered the 'problem' to be within the black community. Racism is a long-endured inhumanity in Toxteth's black community.[20] While the rest of Merseyside and the country talked about the biting recession of the 1970s, the people of Toxteth must have wondered; for they have never been released from its jaws. Recession, in terms of disproportionate unemployment, discrimination in schools, work and housing, minimal social amenities and heavy policing, is an established way of life in the community.

Liverpool's black community is not alone in its experiences of personal and institutionalized white racism.[21] Throughout the 1970s the Community Relations Commission, the Institute of Race

Relations, the Runnymede Trust, the National Council for Civil Liberties and the West Indian Standing Conference produced numerous reports and comment on the effects of institutionalized racism in work, schooling, housing, welfare and policing. On Merseyside, the Area Profile Group and local CRC officers continually presented chilling accounts of racist police practices, intimidation and harassment. From the community, civil rights groups, church groups, politicians and academics the theme was consistent: police-community relations were at crisis point in Britain's black communities. The Select Committee on Race Relations and Immigration, as early as 1971–2, took evidence of this breakdown but the Committee refused to attach any real significance to it.

In 1978 a BBC 'Nationwide' series on the policing of Merseyside broadcast a statement which was supposed to reassure black people that 'policemen in general . . . are not racialist'. The statement, made by BBC reporter Martin Young, and later published in a *Listener* article,[22] considered that the police 'are the first to define the problem of half-castes in Liverpool'. It went on:

> Many are the products of liaisons between black seamen and
> white prostitutes in Liverpool 8, the red-light district.
> Naturally, they do not grow up with any kind of
> recognizable home life. Worse still, after they have done the
> round of homes and institutions, they gradually realize they
> are nothing.

This statement confirmed the worst fears about racist stereotypes and police attitudes. It showed how easy it was for a supposedly non-biased, state-run media to legitimate that very racism. The statement concluded with a challenge to 'pinko, liberal attitudes'. For 'when you are suddenly faced . . . with the stark reality of villainy, when you see the total contempt that the hardened criminal feels for society and the law, you have to think again about the efficiency of the powers we allow the police . . .' There was no questioning of the racism, both implicit and explicit, in the police position, just an acceptance of the tough life faced by the police as the basis for an extension of their powers.

Local people responded angrily to this statement, held a mass meeting and a peaceful demonstration. It brought neither a full apology nor any apparent change in police practices and attitude.

Both in and beyond Toxteth the tensions over lack of protection from white racist aggression,[23] the use of SUS,[24] police harassment[25] and the use of saturation policing[26] were all identified as forming the foundations upon which serious confrontations would be built. By the late 1970s community relations and youth agencies warned that open conflict with the police was imminent in the inner cities. The 1980 Home Affairs Committee on Racial Disadvantage received wide-ranging evidence, in particular from the Merseyside Area Profile Group, that police harassment and aggression towards black youth had become a major cause for concern.

It is hard to believe that the Chief Constable of Merseyside, or any of this fellow senior colleagues in ACPO, were oblivious to the mounting critique of police racist policies and practices. The use of the Special Patrol Group on a regular basis to saturate black communities in London brought scathing criticism from some borough councils concerned about the clear racial discrimination which lay at the heart of the Metropolitan Police strategy of differential policing. Despite the clear wishes of the elected representatives the swamp tactics of saturation continued on the streets. The message was clear: if you were young and black, always leave early for appointments because the chances of being stopped and searched were high. The following were all major criticisms of the Metropolitan Police made by an Unofficial Inquiry into the events in Southall in April 1979:[27] the selective arrests of young Asians; the cordoning off of the centre of the community to allow the fascists to verbally abuse the inhabitants; the writing of National Front symbols by the police on their personnel carriers; the arbitrary use of the truncheon against black people; the killing of Blair Peach and the injuring of many other demonstrators; and the unusually high conviction rate of black people in the magistrates' court on police evidence alone. Again the writing was on the wall.

In his immediate responses to the Toxteth disturbances, the Merseyside Chief Constable attempted to portray the deep-seated conflict as just an outbreak of hooliganism and thieving. It was not a 'race riot', he told the press, 'it was between blacks and the police by a small hooligan and criminal element hellbent on confrontation ... my message to them is that they can't win.'[28] The element of winning and losing a battle was personalized by Oxford during the height of the disturbances. He said of the 'young thugs' involved: 'I don't care whether they are yellow, black or white – they won't beat me.'[29] His determined portrayal of the 'battle' as being one of young hooligans against authority is clear in the following comment:

Parents have a responsibility to discipline and control the movement and behaviour of their children . . . I have no doubt that *we* (the police) are the readily identifiable symbols of authority which are anathema to these people.[30]

So while the actual street violence was in the hands of 'young thugs' or 'black hooligans', the underlying cause, that of a general lawlessness and denial of authority, was at the door of every house in the community. The community, then, was undisciplined, hostile and uncontrollable. On this reasoning the police could not expect the consent of the people because the police, as the reasoning symbols of reasonable authority, were 'anathema' to the life style and values of 'these people'. Institutionalized racism by authority – at its many governmental levels – and the racist practices of policing did not enter the debate. It was down to the black aliens in the midst of white justice and white rationality.

The portrayal of black pathology was substantially added to by sensationalist media exposés of political infiltrators and agitators using the radio networks to co-ordinate strategic attacks on the police. 'Who are the hooded men?' demanded the headlines. A piece in the *Daily Mail* revealed all in an article which linked a Marxist agitator, thought to be involved in the riots, with international terrorist organizations. John Stokes, MP, well known for his right-wing views on immigration, blamed the riots on

. . . the vociferous immigration lobby who seek excuses all the time for the excesses of the blacks . . . Unless the Home Secretary and the police act with the utmost ruthlessness, the once peaceful and ordered life in England will be gone for ever.[31]

With an increasing clamour to use troops, Teddy Taylor, Tory MP for Southend, demanded the introduction of water cannon to clear 'the hooligans and protestors off the streets'. Again the communities could not be seen as acting rationally and politically against their conditions of oppression. They were either at the mercy of political agitators who had come in from outside, or under the control of hardened criminal or hooligan elements within. The climate was established for an aggressive response. If troops were not to be used, then the police would fight fire with fire.

In this climate Oxford admits to a change in tactics from that of 'low-key policing' to what he termed a 'positive police policy'. The community had rejected the former, he argued, the people had 'spat' in his face. His warning was clear: 'Law-abiding people should get off the streets: this is not a Roman carnival.' Once this warning had been voiced the implications were obvious. Anyone who remained 'on the streets' was not considered to be law-abiding. It is not clear as to whether this was directly intended. Certainly it would appear that a curfew had been placed on the Toxteth community. Given the arbitrary nature of police aggression, particularly Merseyside officers, it would appear that mere presence on the streets made individuals legitimate targets. The 'positive strategy' went further. In his report to the Police Committee, Oxford stated that 'it was decided . . . that vehicles should be used in order to get police resources near to the crowd'. Given the death of David Moore and the serious injury to Paul Conroy, both in situations which involved police vehicles in pedestrian areas, it is important to weigh Oxford's words carefully. He stated: 'It was planned to resort to the use of protected vehicles *deployed into the crowd in order to break it up* and wherever possible to arrest the ring leaders.' (Emphasis added.) The offensive use of vehicles as a means of dispersal is well established in the north of Ireland. So too is the use of CS gas.

Oxford justified the use of CS gas as the only means 'to regain control of the streets from the rioters', although he was 'fully aware of the Home Office instructions' which limit the use of CS gas to armed and besieged criminals.[32] He recognized in his report to Scarman that the cartridges used 'were of a type not designed for use in public order situations'.[33] While the officers involved in the use of CS gas 'were all highly trained in the use of firearms, including CS gas launchers', he admitted that this did not 'encompass the control of public order situations'.[34] Using CS gas, or misusing it, was passed off as a necessity in a situation where police officers' lives were judged to be at risk. The serious injuries suffered by people as a result of being hit by canisters occurred in Oxford's judgement as a result of ricochets. The Police Federation considered the misuse of the Ferret cartridges as an 'honest mistake'.[35]

These serious questions of operational judgement formed the basis for criticism of the police response to the disturbances. The Police Committee, however, mindful of the Knowsley affair and of the allegations of police racism over the years in Toxteth, established a working party 'to examine means whereby relationships between the police and the public can be improved'. It had taken major civil disturbances on the streets to examine seriously, at long last, the questions raised both within and outside the community throughout the 1970s. The working party on police/public relationships was set up on 24 July 1981 and, after taking evidence from community groups, professional bodies and the police, it presented its first report on 20 October 1981. Meanwhile the Chief Constable was asked to report on the police handling of the disturbances.

In the heat of the disturbances Oxford denied that the issue was 'racial' but 'exclusively a crowd of black hooligans intent on making life unbearable and indulging in criminal activities'.[36] As noted earlier, he was consistent in maintaining that responsibility for the confrontation was 'exclusively' the behaviour of the black community. He appeared to ignore that many 'rioters' or 'looters' were white, that they were of both sexes and of all ages.

His subsequent report, however, was not produced in the heat of the moment. The Chief Constable and his advisers had had time to reflect and take a more considered view of the events. Perhaps the easy labels of 'lawless', 'irresponsibility', 'indiscipline' and 'hooliganism' would be tempered by the passage of time? His report to the Police Committee, entitled 'Public Disorder on Merseyside: July-August 1981' was just five, typed pages. It focused on the use of CS gas, police tactics, complaints against the police and the prevention of disorder. The main proposals were to introduce foot patrols to police Toxteth, to offer a crash programme of training 'aimed at influencing the attitudes of police officers' and to prevent 'a police over-reaction to incidents occurring within the force and particularly within Toxteth'. This would be done by seeking local acceptance for the proposals prior to their introduction. The Chief Constable then provided a 60-page diary and associated statistics on the disturbances.

A more informative report, also supplied to the Police Committee, was the Chief Constable's evidence to the Scarman Inquiry. It is in this report that he provided his evidence on contemporary Toxteth. Rather than reviewing his position at the time of the disturbances, he attempted to theorize his portrayal of Toxteth as a community of inherent criminality and violence. There was a full chapter on Liverpool's violent history: a city 'beset by problems of violence and public disorder throughout the centuries' in which the 'true Liverpudlian' has an 'aggressive nature' and 'belligerent attitude'.[37] He quoted Ramsey Muir's *History of Liverpool* (1907) which described 'outbreaks of violent public disorder as long ago as 1335'. Without qualification Oxford used Muir to establish 'the turbulent character of the Liverpool populace'. He continued:

> . . . its related dangers, problems – problems which multiplied and were aggravated during the eighteenth and nineteenth centuries by large-scale immigration of Irish, with more than 400,000 entering Liverpool in 1846 and 1847, in the aftermath of the great potato famine . . . enough remained to aggravate the problems of poverty, unemployment and overcrowding, which then, *as now*, were the *breeding ground for violence*. (Emphasis added.)

Then came the 'appreciable numbers of Welsh rural labourers who were attracted to a flourishing city'. He stated that it would be a daunting task 'to enumerate the other foreign nationalities', 'for it has been said that there is no city in the world which finds it necessary to maintain so many consular offices to look after the interests of locally resident foreign *exiles*' (emphasis added). Then after the First World War, he noted a 'remarkable increase in the number of coloured immigrants . . . initially seamen who stayed and married local white girls'. This created the issue of 'mixed race'. These statements are close to those quoted earlier by Martin Young which had caused so much anger in the community. Oxford concluded:

> The black community, like the Chinese, has been a feature of Liverpool life for generations. Each of these communities *brought with them* associated problems, disputes and tensions, which on occasion spilled over into outbreaks of violence. (Emphasis added.)

He then catalogued the street confrontations related to racial conflict and demonstrated that 'Liverpool . . . has for many years fulfilled her [sic] reputation as a tough, violent city, to the present day.' Racism, both at individual and at institutional levels, was not considered. Nowhere was the history of the Merseyside working-class experience, of casual work, of structured unemployment, of poor housing, of discriminating responses of the local state or of the attitudes and policies of the Liverpool police, identified as issues. The 'problems, disputes and tensions' have their roots *within* the immigrant communities, they were brought by them into the city. Inevitably then, Liverpool's people have

> . . . long been reputed to be proportionately tougher, more violent and more pugnacious . . . this belligerent attitude has found expression in violent disturbances similar to . . . the most recent outbreaks in Toxteth.

In Oxford's account the history of religious, race, class and feminist struggle in Liverpool is lost in explanations of violence which are an easy mix of pathological aggression and cultural transmission. In his view, it is a violence, along with other tensions and problems, commonly found within immigrant communities; and it brings a crime problem associated directly with the pathology of these communities. In a chapter on 'Crime' he argues that since 1974 on Merseyside there had been a 74-6 per cent increase in crimes of violence against the person. Most of this crime he locates within the Toxteth community where 'large numbers of ethnic minorities, including blacks' live. The statistics are presented to show Merseyside's 'crime wave' as being based on the Toxteth community. Theft from the person is shown as 'five times greater' and robbery as 'ten times greater' than the national average. The community, referred to as the 'natural homing ground for immigrants', is the base for 'so-called mugging' and the place where 'street prostitution is customary and there is a flourishing drug traffic'.[38]

Thus Liverpool is portrayed as a lawless city whose inhabitants are historically pugnacious by nature and culture. Immigrants are shown as having their own special conflicts and tensions. Young blacks, according to this position, are influenced by being born as Liverpudlians into an inherently violent community. Starting from the statistical evidence, which Oxford argues shows that Merseyside has 'a particularly high incidence of crimes of violence' and that Toxteth 'is the scene for a high proportion of such crime', the allegations of police harassment are virtually dismissed.[39]

Assumptions about Merseyside's negative reputation – particularly the imagery of violence – are given credibility by this kind of narrow, out-of-control account of history. Semi-academic interpretations of 'nature', 'character' and 'attitudes' are married to unquestioned assumptions about the supposed environment ('breeding grounds', 'natural homing ground', 'cultural deficiency') and moral degeneracy, and then applied as *universal* explanations for all acts of violence, public disorder, industrial conflict and crime. This leads not only to policies which react against the communities but also to excesses in police practice being justified on the basis of the 'flawed' community. It is this process of political management – reaction leading to policy decisions which legitimize certain practices – which is central to the argument that racism is deeply institutionalized. Indeed, the policies of selective and discriminatory policing throughout the UK are such that they are the embodiment of institutionalized racism.

It was this very issue that Lord Scarman ducked when he rejected the allegation that Britain is an institutionally racist society. He was satisfied that the racial prejudice which 'does manifest itself occasionally in the behaviour of a few officers on the streets . . . is not to be found amongst senior police officers'.[40] When it comes to the question of racism at a policy level there is a marked reluctance to identify and criticize operational decisions. After the Toxteth disturbances people looked to the Police Committee working party for some judgement concerning the level of racism in policies, priorities and practices.

There was a tacit acceptance, both by the Police Committee and by Scarman, that 'relations between the police and the black community in Toxteth . . . are in a state of crisis'.[41] The terms of reference of the working party reflected this, its objective being 'to examine means whereby relationships between the police and the public can be improved'. Of central concern to the working party was the allegation, 'expressed most vociferously and most often',[42] of police harassment. This included: 'indiscriminate and extensive use of formal "stop and search" procedures'; 'verbal abuse and physical violence on the part of the police'; 'subsequent arrests on the sole charge of assaulting a police officer'; 'overpolicing and/or aggressive policing'. The report dealt with a range of further allegations concerning police attitudes. These included: the tendency to regard large sections of the population as potential criminals or second-class citizens; a general lack of respect for the area's residents and their rights; a lack of understanding of and sympathy for the life style of ethnic groups; and verbal racist abuse. The Police Committee Working Party stated its concern about the disturbing complaints of assault of civilians by the police 'during the course of arrests and in police vehicles and in police stations'.[43] There was considerable dissatisfaction with the complaints procedure, both in terms of internal investigation and 'fear of reprisals'. The Working Party concluded that 'the sheer weight of adverse evidence compels us to recognize that a gulf exists between the police and certain sections of the community in Liverpool 8'.[44]

As mentioned above, the Chief Constable appeared to recognize that some of these allegations were well founded. The proposal to introduce foot patrols was intended to reduce tension, to improve training so as to influence officers' attitudes, and to prevent police overreaction within the community. Each of these proposals reveals some acceptance that the previous system of policing was not all that it should have been, that officers' attitudes and their reactions to events were, at least to some extent, short of the mark. The Police Committee working party recommended a change in police attitudes, a review of the use of stop and search, a reduction in the level of aggressive policing, a greater understanding of the problems within the community and a more positive role for the police in the community. In keeping with the Scarman recommendations, it argued for a community-policing model which would put more officers on the streets in direct contact with the community and, accordingly, a new programme of police training. A further recommendation in line with Scarman was to establish a structure for police-community consultation. This would take the form of consultation centres within the community 'as a forum for an exchange of views between those concerned with policing and the consumer'.[45] 'Those concerned' were identified as police authority members, the police, community groups and professional agencies. These proposals were not unique. They were adopted and developed by Chief Constable John Alderson in Devon and Cornwall as the cornerstone of his community-policing model and they were to gain wider acceptance following the Scarman recommendations.

The national impact of Scarman and the local direction of the Police Committee working party led to a commitment to 'a programme designed to promote mutual support and understanding'. The programme was accepted by the Chief Constable. It included the provision of information and reassurance on current policing policies and police authority decisions; the improvement of the 'free flow of information' between the police, the police committee and the public; the setting up of procedures and facilities for community consultation; a report on the extensive allegations of police harassment and the alleged misuse of stop and search; the remodelling of basic training for police officers. The revitalized public face of Merseyside's police was soon revealed nationwide as the new-style community beat officers posed for the press and television. The reality in Toxteth was quite different as a high police presence persisted, as did the regular skirmishes between groups of people and police officers on the streets.

The 1981 disturbances continued to have major implications for national policy decisions. In reply to a question in the House, the then Home Secretary, William Whitelaw, revealed that recommendations on police riot clothing and equipment had been received from a parliamentary working group set up after the Brixton disturbances of April 1981 and circulated to all chief constables and police authorities. The working group had already been constituted at the time of the disturbances, and 'against the background of events on Merseyside', where CS gas had been used as a 'last resort', Whitelaw added a further dimension to the group's work. It was to consider 'sophisticated and offensive anti-riot weapons *as well as purely protective* measures'. At the time of the Bristol disturbances in 1980 the police had been so vulnerable that a company making cricket boxes had sold out of its entire stock. The parliamentary working group had been reviewing all forms of protective equipment but the post-Toxteth directive extended this to the already controversial plastic bullets and CS gas. While it had doubts over the utility of water cannon, it recommended that chief constables should use their discretion.

It was this working group's opinion, restated by Whitelaw, that offensive weaponry such as CS gas and plastic bullets should be restricted in their use to situations of 'last resort'. There is no statement as to what constitutes 'last resort'. Curiously, however, both Oxford and Whitelaw used the term 'last resort' to describe the use of CS gas in Toxteth. On this basis, had plastic bullets and water cannon been used in Toxteth then, under the Home Secretary's new recommendations, they would have been quite acceptable. Establishing what constitutes a situation of 'last resort', who defines it as such and how decisions are then made operationally are crucial issues. This is particularly disturbing given the death of so many people in the north of Ireland from injuries inflicted by plastic bullets.

Although Oxford was admonished by the Merseyside Police Committee for his unauthorized expenditure of £56,000, and many serious questions concerning his wrongful use of Ferret CS gas, the offensive use of vehicles and individual complaints remained unanswered, it appears that the definition of Toxteth as a situation of 'last resort' justified all the police responses. From criticisms of serious errors of judgement in the police handling of the Toxteth disturbances the position changed to one in which Toxteth was elevated to a blueprint for future situations of 'last resort'.

Undermining a chief constable?

The tragedy is that in their genuine wish to strengthen local government ties and protect the public purse, enthusiastic democrats will open the door to those whose sole aim is political direction and control of the police and the removal of independence and power from chief constables. The warning bells are now ringing.[46]

This statement, made by Greater Manchester's Chief Constable, James Anderton, summarizes well the general police response at all levels to the interventions of police committee members in controversial issues. It appears that whenever police authorities attempt to call their chief constables to account they are portrayed as engaging in an exercise in *control* rather than *accountability*. Furthermore, it seems totally acceptable to Anderton that chief constables' *powers* should be *independent* of the democratic process.

Nowhere has this position been more apparent than in the relationship between the GLC and the Metropolitan Police. In 1981 the first-ever socialist Labour group were elected to power on the GLC. With the Metropolitan Police the only force outside the structure of political accountability, it was clear that there would be a considerable struggle to reform the law and establish an official police committee for the GLC. The media's obsession with the personal life and political associations of the GLC leader, Ken Livingstone, and the portrayal of Labour rule as a front for an 'extremist' takeover brought all new proposals under scrutiny and attack. Consequently, the mild proposal to bring the Met. into line with other police forces – the so-called 'democratization' of the Met. – was criticized as a 'leftist' plot to undermine police powers and operational control.

What had begun with two confrontations over accountability on Merseyside, the policing of Knowsley and the handling of the Toxteth uprising, had become the 'proof' of political subversion of police powers. At a Merseyside Police Federation Conference late in 1981 the Federation Chairman, James Jardine, mounted a scathing attack on the local police committee:

> I find it incredible that a police authority can see what
> happened in Liverpool this summer, and then embark on a
> sustained campaign of denigration against its own force. I
> find it disgusting that elected leaders, charged with the
> responsibility of protecting the whole of the community,
> seek to undermine the position of their own chief
> constable.[47]

This position was developed further by Fred Jones, the Merseyside Police Federation leader, who stated that the Police Committee had no business involving itself with issues of an operational nature. The requests for information and the calling for reports by the Police Committee in both the Knowsley and Toxteth cases were clearly within the letter of the 1964 Police Act. Given the seriousness of the issues and the massive local, community-based concern, it could be argued that had the Police Committee not intervened and called for reports it would have failed in its statutory duties.

Several months after the Greater Manchester Police Committee had raised questions with their Chief Constable over his handling of the 1981 disturbances in Moss Side, further concern was voiced over his response to a local strike. A Manchester engineering company, Laurence Scott, was in dispute with its workers and had been effectively picketed for some time. Eventually the strikebound factory experienced an 'SAS-style' raid in which balaclava-clad men were dropped by helicopter and essential supplies were airlifted out of the factory. The size of the operation, the effective breaking of the strike and the police involvement brought extensive criticism from many sources; these issues are discussed further in Chapter 7. The Police Committee made their criticism known about the handling of the Laurence Scott affair. Anderton's response was to come down hard on political intervention. He said:

> I sense and see in our midst an enemy more dangerous, insidious and ruthless than any faced since the Second World War. I firmly believe that there is a long-term political strategy to destroy the proven structure of the police and turn them into an exclusive agency of a one-party state. I am also convinced that the police service is now a prime target for subversion and demonstration. The people must not be tricked into dropping their guard or their standards, and chief constables must ensure that their forces are not infiltrated by undesirable people who could wreak havoc in the year ahead.[48]

Much of what James Anderton is quoted as saying, and he has spoken with some regularity throughout the late 1970s on a wide range of issues, is portrayed as heat-of-the-moment responses of a slightly eccentric chief constable. Yet rarely is his comment constructed spontaneously. He speaks with careful preparation, he is articulate and well-organized. It is clear that he catches the mood and temperature of popular opinion and articulates what many people think about race, law and order, punishment, morality, Victorian values and the rest. It is the fact that he is a 'people's' chief constable – the mouthpiece of popularly held prejudices – that demands that he be taken seriously. While many of his colleagues in ACPO might occasionally dissassociate themselves from his tactics or style, they share his position, particularly with regard to any possible extension of the effective powers or responsibilities of police authorities.

The confrontations between the police committees of Merseyside and Greater Manchester and their chief constables were tempered initially by a defence taken from the 1964 Police Act. While police authorities have primary responsibility for securing an adequate and efficient police force for their area, they have no effective control over what happens on the streets. If they care to see events on the street as undefined, ambiguous situations of 'last resort', chief constables can use their political autonomy to settle civil disorder by means of plastic bullets, CS gas and even water cannon. While this has been resisted in some areas by police committees refusing to allocate resources for the purchase of offensive weaponry, there is no doubt, after Whitelaw's response to Toxteth, that should the occasion arise, the use of such equipment will be left to the discretion of the chief constable. As with Toxteth, supplies will be made available from other sources.

Having defended their autonomy through the law, the chief constables, supported by the Police Federation, moved onto the offensive. They reverted to the imagery of the 'enemy within' – democracy threatened by subversives, agitators and extremists. The final insult to people like Margaret Simey, who has given many years of service to local government, was that if people like her were not extremists themselves, they were putty in the hands of the militants. In other words, the 'democratic process' and its elected representatives are acceptable as long as they remain in line with police thinking; opposition is a betrayal of democracy. The conclusion to be drawn from the Merseyside example is how far political opinion remains tempered by attempts to accommodate, if not placate, the police offensive. The way in which this process of accommodation operates was demonstrated by events which followed the crisis in police accountability on Merseyside.

The Labour Party in Merseyside's Granby ward – the area which had experienced much of the police-community confrontation of the 1970s and the 1981 disturbances – held extensive discussions about policing with individuals and organizations in Liverpool, Birmingham and London. As a result of these discussions it published a pamphlet entitled 'Policing in a Democracy: Proposals for Reform' which considered critically the 'problems of policing in a democratic society'. The issues, as far as the authors are concerned, were clear:

> There is widespread concern that the police have come to
> see themselves as a separate and unaccountable body.

Certainly the large numbers of people who are engaged in violent confrontation make this gulf a blatant fact. Yet far too often the police react defensively, describing critics as being purely politically or even criminally motivated, and retreat into operational policies which, while prestigious, remove them further from the public they serve. This siege mentality of the police has produced accusations of even mild reforms being 'anti-police'. This confuses the debate still further . . . In the area there is widespread distrust of the police, especially evident amongst young blacks. The reasons lie in a history of police racism, malpractice, harassment and provocation . . . the power the law gives the police and the way in which it is abused makes this racism a particularly dangerous poison.[49]

The Granby Labour Group, which has among its councillors Margaret Simey and the Merseyside Labour leader, Bill Hamilton, argued for an 'entire shift in the way the police force operates'. As representatives of the Toxteth community, these councillors clearly accepted the allegations of racial harassment and aggressive policing which had been made extensively to the Police Committee working party. The question of political accountability could only be resolved by 'the responsibility for *overall control, organization* and *policy decisions* of the police force' being placed in the hands of 'the democratically elected representatives of the community that the police serve'. The Labour Group concluded that changes in the law were essential to bring the police under democratic control:

Police authorities should have more powers to determine police policy and practice upon such matters as: deployment, community liaison, discipline, recruitment, attitudes, police training, equipment and spending. The authority should *not* have the power to interfere with individual prosecutions but all matters affecting the manner, quality and type of policing in an area must be considered legitimate areas for the authority to declare policy upon.[50]

The Group proposed the setting-up of community police councils which would make recommendations to the police authority concerning the policing of their communities. The police would be legally obliged to consult with the CPCs on all matters which had any bearing on police operations in their areas.

On the 20 October 1981 a resolution was passed unanimously which committed the Merseyside Police Committee 'to a programme designed to promote mutual support and understanding as the sole basis on which a police force can operate'. The programme directed the police authority to discuss with the Chief Constable 'ways in which the existing arrangements for the free flow of information between the authority, the police and the public might be improved'. To that end it directed that 'some appropriate form of community consultative machinery be set up on a neighbourhood basis'.

In December 1981 the working party on police/public relationships recommended further that the Police Committee should set up 'a "Police Consultation" in Toxteth consisting of representatives of the police authority, the police, community organizations and the professional bodies'. The framework of consultation established was directly compatible with that initiated by John Alderson's community-policing model in Devon and Cornwall. However, it remained some distance from the initiative proposed by the Granby Labour Party. Rather than providing police authorities with powers to determine operational policies and priorities and insisting that the police should be accountable to the communities they serve for their operational practices and interventions, it placed responsibility in the hands of other professionals – such as teachers, social workers, the clergy, etc. It replaced the objective of effective accountability with discretionary consultation. It provided a good example of the real limits on effective proposals for change.

Nevertheless, the Merseyside confrontations over police powers and accountability reveal a quite different form of police committee from the benign image discussed at the opening of this chapter. Gradually, from being very much a lone voice of opposition to the Chief Constable, Margaret Simey's critique of his political autonomy was taken up by others on the Committee. There was no lack of political commitment in the aftermath of the events in Knowsley and Toxteth. In these cases, as in Great Manchester, the Chief Constable was put under considerable, consistent and informed pressure by councillors with a deep sense of public responsibility. While their persistence certainly made the Chief Constable's job more difficult and brought about some changes of emphasis in police strategy, training and deployment, it clearly failed to instigate any important structural changes in terms of accountability. Furthermore, for their trouble, the Police Committee members who criticized their chief constables' decisions were severely dealt with in the media. Yet they had presented quite reasonable cases about very serious issues of public concern. That they were pilloried publicly by individual chief constables and by the police organizations served as a warning to other police committee members who might decide to criticize their chief officers.

In this long-drawn-out conflict many of the central, specific issues were lost, many of the serious questions raised by disturbing individual cases remain unanswered and the police emerged formally unscathed but with their so-called community-based strategies in tatters. Yet, throughout the political conflict the Chief Constable of Merseyside, like his colleague in Greater Manchester, never once abused or misused his powers under the 1964 Police Act. If they did anything at all, they showed just how extensive and permissive are the powers of chief constables. It is also important not to over-represent the criticism of chief constables by police authorities. For the most part, police committees remain wholly supportive of their chief constables, are quick to defend all kinds of possible excesses and to deny any conflict of interest. Fundamentally, little has changed and the agenda, content and decisions of police committee procedures still remain firmly in the grasp of the chief constables.

Following the establishment of the 'partnership policing' programme on Merseyside, which set its hopes on a network of community-liaison forums, relations between the Police Committee and the Merseyside Police improved. As Chapter 7 shows, however, the police response to the coal dispute early in 1984 shattered any trust that had been built up and the Chief Constable once again came into serious conflict with the Police Committee.

5. Scarman: a diversionary interlude

> The first few months after Scarman were crazy. I was sent down to talk to groups of PCs about community relations and their attitude to the coloureds. They didn't know why they were there and I didn't know what I was supposed to tell them. What I do know is that they resented being there. They felt that they were being blamed. Personally . . . I mean. They took it badly. After all a lot of their mates had been injured at Toxteth and Moss Side . . . and they'd never even been there before . . . (Training School Sergeant, 1983)

Race, public order and policing – the Scarman Report

In the controversy over community relations and police racism which came to dominate the 'public debate' following the 1982 Scarman Report various important issues were lost sight of: the issues of operational policy decisions, the selection of priorities and the institutional acceptance of aggressive if not brutal practices. To a great extent this has suited the police. It shifted the focus away from questions about the police as an institution to the safer area of the personal attitudes and prejudices of individual police officers and their relationships with the black community.

At the Home Secretary's request, Lord Scarman, a member of the Judicial Committee of the House of Lords, was appointed to conduct an inquiry into the 'Brixton Disorders of 10-12 April 1981'. The media coverage given to the Scarman Report was extraordinary by any standards. It dominated the news for over a week and became the central focus of special features and documentaries for months. Scarman took evidence from a broad range of sources (he visited the West Midlands and Merseyside) and he argued that the 'Brixton disorders' had to be viewed in a wider context. Nevertheless, his actual inquiry was restricted to

Brixton, the local black community and the Metropolitan Police. The media and other commentators, including left academics, have generalized the Scarman Report and the analysis of the Brixton experience, extending its relevance to other cities and communities. This has served to legitimize and reinforce the Report as a definitive statement on police-community relations.

Lord Scarman produced a series of recommendations very similar to those made by the Merseyside Police Committee Working Group into Police-Community Relations. They focused on five areas. Firstly, recommendations on recruitment: there should be more recruits from ethnic minorities and new 'scientific' methods detecting racism should be used at the recruitment stage. Secondly, recommendations on training: these included the expansion of the basic training programme for new recruits with an emphasis on race awareness training, and the development of in-service training programmes emphasizing community relations and the handling of public disorder. Thirdly, recommendations about supervision and responsibility: these emphasized in particular the development of management skills. Fourth, and most controversial, was the recommendation that 'racially prejudiced behaviour' should incur immediate dismissal from the force. Finally, with regard to police methods and practices, patrol patterns should be established in which home beat officers would be used to develop a programme of community policing. The success of such a programme would depend on closer involvement by the police with the community, longer continuity of deployment and a broader age-range of officers working in the community.

Central to Lord Scarman's proposals for promoting stronger links between the community and the police was the recommendation that consultative or liaison committees should be set up. In Paragraph 5.56 of the Report he stated that 'community involvement in the policy and operations of policing is perfectly feasible without undermining the independence of the police or destroying the secrecy of those operations against crime which have to be kept secret'. While his reaffirmation of the independence of the police is instructive, he went on to argue that consultation and accountability are essential mechanisms in the provision of relevant and responsible policing within the community. Although he stressed the importance of accountability and its status as a 'constitutional mechanism' – the 'key to successful consultation and socially responsive policing' – he did not address the crisis in political accountability. What he did recommend was the establishment, by the police, of statutory liaison committees or other consultative machinery. He concluded:

> Community representatives must seek to appreciate the
> difficulties (and dilemmas) of the police, and to avoid
> extravagant language or ill-formed criticism. If, as I believe
> to be essential, a relationship of mutual trust and respect is
> to be fostered between local communities and the police,
> both sides will have to be prepared to give and take and to
> work positively to establish and maintain such a
> relationship. (Para. 5.71)

Within this framework, however, the police were not obliged to respond to the demands of the community. The recommendations moved no nearer to guaranteeing people any effective say in the policing of their communities.

The weight of Scarman's argument was directed at the issue of race. This is apparent early in the Report where he stated:

> Two views have been forcibly expressed in the course of the
> Inquiry into the causation of the disorders. The first is:
> oppressive policing over a period of years, and in particular
> the harassment of young blacks on the streets of Brixton . . .
> The second is that the disorders, like so many riots in
> British history, were a protest against society by people,
> deeply frustrated and deprived, who saw in a violent attack
> upon the forces of law and order their one opportunity of
> compelling public attention to their grievances.[1]

Scarman dismissed these two positions as 'oversimplifications' and went on to locate the 'policing problem' as being derived in 'policing a multiracial community where unemployment, especially among young black people, is high and hopes are low'. The 'policing problem' can only be understood, according to Scarman, within the context of the 'social problem'. He stated;

> I identify the social problem as that of the difficulties, social
> and economic, which beset the ethnically diverse

communities who live and work in our inner cities. These
are difficulties for which the police bear no responsibility,
save as citizens, like the rest of us. But, unless the police
adjust their policies and operations so as to handle these
difficulties with imagination as well as firmness, they will
fail: and disorder will become a disease endemic in our
society.[2]

Scarman was adamant in his refusal to accept charges of
institutionalized racism. While he accepted that 'unintentional'
discrimination existed in some local authority services and that
'practices may be adopted by public bodies . . . which are
unwittingly discriminatory against black people', he argued that
Britain is not an institutionally racist society.[3]

It was, however, Scarman's conclusion that racism exists within
the Metropolitan Police. But, like the Merseyside Police Committee
Working Group and its Chief Constable, Kenneth Oxford, Scarman
considered police racism to be isolated to a minority of young police
officers. He argued that their racism was an unfortunate product of
bad screening in recruitment and inadequate training. It was on this
basis that Scarman recommended changes in recruitment and
training and that officers be dismissed for 'racially prejudiced acts'.
Any question that racism could be considered a common
characteristic throughout police policies and operations was
dismissed. Criticism that the 'Metropolitan Police is a racist police
force' with the 'integrity and impartiality of its senior direction . . .
severely challenged' drew the following reply from Scarman:

The direction and policies of the Metropolitan Police are not
racist. I totally and unequivocally reject the attack made
upon the integrity and impartiality of the senior direction of
the force . . . The allegation that the police are the
oppressive arm of a racist state not only displays a complete
ignorance of the constitutional arrangements for controlling
the police: it is an injustice to the senior officers of the
force.[4]

The fault lay elsewhere: 'in errors of judgement, in a lack of
imagination and flexibility, but *not* in deliberate bias or prejudice'.
'Racial prejudice', according to Scarman, was an occasional

occurrence 'of a few officers on the streets'. Even these moments of racism were perceived as 'lapses':

> It may be only too easy for some officers, faced with what they must see as the *inexorably rising tide of street crime*, to lapse into an *unthinking assumption* that all young black people are potential criminals . . . The damage done by even the *occasional* display of racial prejudice is incalculable. It goes far to the creation of an *image* of a hostile police force, which was the myth which led young people into these disorders. (Emphasis added)

Scarman's carefully weighed words were instructive. He accepted without question that street crime in the area was an 'inexorably rising tide'. This was then unconsciously transmitted into the minds of young, inexperienced police officers as an 'unthinking assumption' that it must be black youth who were riding the crest of the tidal wave. Isolated cases of police harassment and prejudice occurred which were then portrayed as generalized police hostility towards young blacks. The black population then simply embarked on a riotous response directed against their mythical oppressors. Throughout Scarman's account the position is consistent: police racism is an aberration based on the unthinking and quite understandable actions of a handful of young officers. Any possibility that racism might constitute an ideology which penetrated all levels of police direction and operations was discounted as a mischievous and extreme rhetoric.

'Operation Swamp', one of a series of saturation policing interventions in the London Borough of Lambeth, immediately preceded the Brixton uprising. Not only had saturation policing long been deeply resented within the black community, it was also rejected by many local authorities in Greater London. Faced with overwhelming evidence of the contribution of Operation Swamp to the disturbances, Scarman argued that it was not saturation policing in areas of identifiable high crime which was the problem. Rather, in the case of Brixton, an error of judgement had been made in its *timing*. This was in line with Scarman's overall conclusion that there was little wrong with policy, just occasional lapses in practice.

Scarman's criticisms of the police could easily be handled by implementing his recommendations on recruitment and training.

New courses, particularly focusing on 'human awareness training', soon emerged throughout the main police forces. Within a year courses in community relations training were in full operation and a new centre for police studies was announced for Brunel University.

Despite Scarman's tendency to ignore central issues, such as the crisis in political accountability and institutionalized racism, the police smarted from his criticisms. His recommendations for greater community consultation drew a typically aggressive response from James Anderton. The Chief Constable of Greater Manchester stated that if Scarman's proposals were introduced, 'the character of the British police would be changed for ever and life in this country would never be the same again'. He argued that the 'survival of the country' was at stake and that it would be determined in the city areas where race was a major factor. Anderton's position drew immediate support from James Jardine, then Chairman of the Police Federation.

It was Scarman's explicit acceptance of the existence of a 'wave' of street crime and his view that it centred on black communities which created space for the police to build their backlash. In early March 1982, just three months after the publication of the Scarman Report, figures were leaked through the *London Evening Standard* which claimed a 96 per cent increase in muggings. And for the first time the police specified the ethnic origin of the alleged attackers. The *Standard* argued that Scarman's recommendations would hinder effective policing. Joe Sim states that at a Home Affairs Committee of Conservative MPs Scarman was 'bitterly criticized for himself criticizing policing methods in Brixton'. The charge was that he had transformed a 'straightforward issue of crime into one of race relations'. According to Sim,

> When Scotland Yard held a press conference the following day, the press and media were primed and ready to hear the news about black muggers. For their part, the Yard were also ready. By using the crime figures, built around the stereotype of the black male mugger, they were about to confront Scarman's challenge to their power and autonomy.[5]

Scotland Yard stated there were 18,763 offences of robbery and other violent theft in 1981, of which 10,399 offences were allegedly committed by 'non-whites'. The figures were used not only to justify saturation policing and other hard-line clampdowns on 'black crime' but implicitly to attack Scarman and the weakness of the Home Secretary. It was Scarman's description of the 'inexorably rising tide of street crime' which presented the police with an open invitation to move their race statistics into the forefront of the debate. The media lost no time in pursuing the issue of race just as had happened during the first 'mugging panic' of 1973.[6] 'Black crime' re-emerged as headline news for several weeks after the release of the statistics. The Scarman Report and the Metropolitan Police criminal statistics put race highest on the agenda of concern over policing the 1980s.

Race, crime and policing – the 'Left realist' response

Arguing their concern for the problems which crime and its growth inflicted on working-class communities and the lack of effective policing in those communities, John Lea and Jock Young, two radical academics, presented what they termed a 'Left realist', as opposed to a 'Left idealist', response to the issues of crime and policing. As with Scarman, the issue of race remained central to their analysis. They argued:

> What we are witnessing among 'West Indian' black youth is the development of a counterculture, a culture of discontent resulting precisely from the visibility of deprivation, a visibility highlighted by the very process of integration into British standards and expectations of life . . . Hustling is not the pursuit of angels. Cultures which grow out of adversity and oppression are as likely to be predatory as progressive. Crime abounds in such communities and whereas most of it is of no significance (e.g. cannabis smoking) other elements such as street robbery and interpersonal violence is seriously antisocial.[7]

Lea and Young ignore the long history of immigration and the deep tradition of white racism at both personal and institutional levels. For them the issue is race and crime and it is located in 'the first generation of immigrants entering this country in the 1950s and 1960s'. They brought with them 'lower expectations of life' because of the conditions which prevailed in their country of origin. Lower expectations guaranteed compliance and an acceptance of white racism.

The 'second generation' are in a quite different position, according to Lea and Young, for they have been 'born in this country to immigrant parents, educated to be equal in job expectations by the school, and in consumer demands by the mass media'. Seeing itself as 'manifestly unequal', West Indian youth has failed to succeed in 'assimilation to indigenous British standards and aspirations' and it is in this process that a 'culture of discontent' has been formed. It is a process brought about by the emphasis on 'homogenization' rather than the 'separateness' of cultures. The resulting 'counterculture of despair and resistance to discrimination and deprivation . . . involves soaring rates of street crime'.

Lea and Young used the police evidence to Scarman in support of this proposition, further reinforced by an unquestioning acceptance of police statistics for mugging and footpad robbery. Their explanation is as inaccurate as is the one provided by the Chief Constable of Merseyside set out in Chapter 4. While their analyses might differ in emphasis, both explanations take for granted that the main issue is the disproportionate involvement of blacks in serious street crime and interpersonal violence. It is this incorrect assumption which then underpins, as with Scarman, the breakdown in the relationship between black youth and the police. Lea and Young argue that it has resulted in a 'vicious circle whereby relations between the police and the community deteriorate in such a way that each step in deterioration increases pressure for deterioration.' They believe that this spiral of deterioration has brought a collapse in the tradition of policing by consent in the inner city. The scenario can be summarized as follows: rising long-term unemployment produces high crime rates which leads to 'high profile' strategies of policing. The community becomes increasingly alienated from the police, 'bystanders' or people not directly involved, become 'mobilized' and there is a refusal to co-operate or to provide information. With their contacts withdrawn, the police are forced to use saturation tactics in selected communities. The street temperature rises and the community responds to specific instances of arrest. 'Riot is on the agenda.' It is the inexorable logic of economic deprivation, underachievement and collapse of consensus policing.

In these accounts serious questions remain unanswered – in fact some have not even been asked. Given that long-term unemployment, underachievement and poverty constitute the daily experience of many predominantly white working-class communities, why should it be that 'riot is on the agenda' only in black communities? For police officers like Oxford the answer is self-evident; it is the 'associated tensions' brought with immigrant culture, particularly the 'volatile' West Indians, which come to the surface in the form of crime and violence. For Lea and Young the answer lies in the 'political marginalization' of second-generation West Indian youth. The problem is confined to West Indian youth because Asian youth has been insulated from the cycle of deprivation. In Lea and Young's analysis the Asian community has substantial economic opportunities derived from hard work, professional and enter-preneurial activities. They incorrectly assume that there is an homogenous Asian culture and that it poses few problems for young UK-born Asians whereas the tensions which exist within cultures are many. The struggles of Asian youth, particularly young women, are glossed over in a simple generalized picture: 'The distance between Asian culture and indigenous British culture is greater than the distance between the West Indian and the indigenous British culture.' The argument is that because West Indian culture and indigenous British culture have more in common with each other than Asian culture, young West Indians feel the strain of failure to a greater extent; enter the 'counterculture'. This position also assumes that there is an indigenous British culture. Is the assumption that the long-term white unemployed can accommodate the reality of their failure to obtain a job of any sort because they are part of one big, protective, white, happy family?

At the base of Lea and Young's analysis lies the dislocation of second-generation West Indian youth. How does this explain the long-endured confrontations between the police and blacks of all ages in communities such as Toxteth and Moss Side, where indigenous black communities are well established? Implicit in most police accounts, supported by Lea and Young, is an almost universal tradition of policing by consent. How does this square with the long history of confrontation and regulation conducted by the police against working-class communities? In their analysis there is no conception of the ways in which black communties have been discriminted against by the police, no reference to the strategies of selective law enforcement and the targeting of particular groups. The implicit assumption is that until recently the police have maintained a consistent presence regardless of neighbourhood reputation, class or race.

Lea and Young have carefully balanced the 'causes' of the crisis in the inner city – what they refer to as 'the vicious circle of the collapse of consensus policing, discrimination and deprivation'. The 'counterculture' has emerged as a response to West Indian youth's failure to achieve the standards of the 'indigenous white culture'. Its resistance, in the tradition of the lumpen proletariat, is found in the rising level of street crime. Black youth has turned in on its own community. It has been street crime which has brought the 'shift to military policing'. This accords with Scarman who considers that these developments are so apparent that the racism of young offenders is quite understandable. Military policing, say Lea and Young, has alienated the black community further, to the point where more people have become involved against the police and there has been a refusal to co-operate with investigations. Consequently, the 'basis of consensus policing' has collapsed. In turn this has brought consolidation to the shift towards military policing and so the circular process has been completed.

It is quite unjustified to claim that real or effective consensus policing has ever existed in working-class neighbourhoods. The earlier chapters of this book exposed this particular myth. To return to Phil Cohen's phrase, the history of policing the inner city is one of a 'grudging acceptance'. Secondly, racism is institutionalized and not simply a new idea confined to a minority of inexperienced police officers. Chapter 4 illustrated both the extent and history of racism in the policing of the black community on Merseyside. The very fact that years of reports, research and parliamentary evidence have been disregarded by senior officers as indicating any cause for concern is sufficient indictment of the depth of racism within the police. Selective forms of policing are found in the early operational practices of the nineteenth-century police based on crude images of criminality. These were largely class images but were easily transferable to racist stereotypes – initially London's Irish population. Thirdly, the uprisings were not an abberation. Yet Scarman and Lea and Young represent them as a breakdown in consensual policing and, therefore, a breakdown in social control.

It is not unusual during crises in the political economy for communities, particularly those at the economic margin, to resist through political protest and industrial conflict. The law has been used consistently to break such forms of protest and the police are the front line of this response. The added dimension of the 1980–1 uprisings was that of institutionalized racism intensified selectively in black communities throughout the seventies. There is no doubt that a most significant moment in the final breakdown of police-community relations came in 1979 in Southall when the police prevented free movement on the streets in order to allow the fascist National Front to demonstrate its racism against the black residents.

Institutionalized racism and the police: the PSI Report

Unlawful police raids on private houses, the use of force in policing sensitive demonstrations and the fabrication of evidence are not only to be seen as serious allegations against individual officers. They are also serious charges against those responsible for the actions of those officers. It is this connection which Scarman failed to make. Consequently, race and police racism has become a diversion in the sense that the debate has centred on the specific actions of individual officers.

In September 1976 no fewer than 17 officers raided the London home of black, 60-year-old couple, David and Lucille White. The raid was mounted supposedly for stolen goods – although none were ever found. The police entry was illegal as they had no search warrant. David White, a slight and frail man, was very seriously beaten and had to take nine weeks off work. The Whites were prosecuted – and subsequently acquitted on charges of assaulting the police. In a private action brought by the Whites against the police in April 1982 Mr Justice Mars-Jones awarded £51,392 to the Whites for 'a catalogue of violence and inhuman conduct by young officers'. He commented: 'I regret to say that I am forced to the conclusion that there had been an orchestrated attempt to mislead the court in order to cover up illegality and unjustified use of force.' This is a very serious conclusion, given subsequent events.

Forced to mount an internal inquiry because of the judge's criticisms and his damages award, the police inquiry focused solely on the events around the actual assault. In February 1984, Scotland Yard 'offered sincere apologies and regret' to the Whites for the 'improper way it dealt with them in the incident'. One officer who admitted to using 'unnecessary violence', a phrase which suggests that some violence was necessary, was fined an undisclosed amount. There was no suggestion that any cover-up, presumably extensive and at a senior level, was investigated. To add insult to injury, the delay in hearing the Whites' action was used by the DPP as a justification not to prosecute the police.

The case raises fundamental questions about the primacy of legal accountability, so often argued by the police. Illegal entry by a posse of officers, a brutal beating, wrongful arrests and, according to the judge, lies to the High Court resulted in a fine for one officer and a letter of apology. The responsibilities of senior officers were never in question.

The intensity of feeling aroused by a succession of race-related cases, of which the brutality inflicted upon the Whites was the most horrific, is clear from the controversy which developed around the death of Colin Roach in Stoke Newington police station. On 13 January 1983 Colin Roach, a young local black, was killed by a shotgun blast at the police station. There was immediate local concern about how Colin Roach had met his death, and demonstrations were held at Stoke Newington police station during the week of his death followed by marches through to May. The Community Alliance for Police Accountability (CAPA) reported that during this period over 90 people were arrested, 127 charges brought against them and 68 convictions made.[8] The GLC journal, *Policing London*, stated:

> According to eyewitness accounts and photographic
> evidence, the police wildly overestimated both the numbers
> and the violence of the demonstrations in order to justify
> their aggressive response and indiscriminate arrests . . . It
> appears from the way the marches were policed, the
> brutality and arbitrary nature of some of the arrests and
> from the way people were handled in local police stations
> that there was a strong element of punishment in police
> behaviour.[9]

The police conduct – their handling of the demonstration, their use of their powers of arrest and the level of force administered – thus became a major issue in itself.

On 20 June 1983, at the inquest into the death of Colin Roach, the ten-person jury, five white and five black jurors, returned a verdict of suicide by an eight-to-two majority. In an unprecedented move the jury wrote a letter to the Home Secretary, Leon Brittan, which included the following passage:

> As members of the jury, and having heard all the evidence in question, we fairly reached a decision of suicide but are deeply distressed at the handling of the case by the police regarding the Roach family. We feel that the bereaved family were kept in the dark over the death of their son – and that the police were not sympathetic to the situation. We also feel that the case could have been investigated more professionally and extensively.

This extraordinary indictment of the police by an inquest jury added substantially to concern in the local community. It emphasized that the case had been mishandled and that the police had operated with disregard for the family. Taken together with the CAPA report, the evidence overwhelmingly suggested that there was a serious case to answer, again at a senior level. In April 1984 Scotland Yard announced that following a thorough investigation into the case no disciplinary action was to be taken against any officers.

In both these cases the issues went well beyond the personal behaviour and prejudices of individual officers and extended to the response of senior officers. The police were criticized in the courts for their handling of the situation. These cases are typical examples of how deeply racism as an ideology is rooted in contemporary police work. Yet Lord Scarman strongly denied such claims and Lea and Young dismiss them as the claims of 'Left idealists'.

In November 1983, however, evidence indicating the depth and significance of institutionalized racism was provided when an independent report, commissioned by the Metropolitan Police, was published by the Policy Studies Institute (PSI). Following persistent criticism about the state of relations between the police and black people in London, the Metropolitan Police Commissioner, Sir David McNee, commissioned the study in 1979. Initially the project was to have been given to John Brown of the Cranfield Institute of Technology, who had published a similar study on the Handsworth area of Birmingham. This earlier report, *Shades of Grey*, closely associated black people with criminality. In 1979

Brown's association with the Met. project was severed as black community leaders were 'unwilling to co-operate with the Cranfield researchers, because they were dissatisfied with the previous projects carried out by the Institute'.[10]

In November 1979 the PSI took over the two-year research project. The brief was extended to cover relationships between the wider community and the police, and to consider a range of attitudes within the police. The study began in 1980 and was organized in four separate sections: a survey of over 2,000 Londoners; an in-depth observation study of a group of young black people; a survey of 1,770 police officers; an in-depth observation and interview study of police work throughout the two years. The aim was to contextualize 'how the police actually behave' and 'how people respond' within the broader structural framework of police operations: management, supervision, objectives, discipline, training, and so on. Also of central importance was the analysis of the daily practices and habits of the police officers, particularly with regard to their 'view of the world' in which they operated, their prejudices and their attitudes. By placing these issues within the context of the police as an institution, they were now to be addressed in a form which Lord Scarman had neglected but which was made imperative by the experiences typified in the White and Roach cases.

Late in 1982, while the PSI study was still in process, Sir David McNee published selections from his retirement memoirs in the *Sunday Mirror*. One of his regrets was that as Commissioner he had failed 'to halt the sniping of critics who seemed determined to sap the morale of the Metropolitan Police.' He concluded:

I am also pleased that the Policy Studies Institute project is well under way, for this is the first in-depth examination of police and public relations and of the requirements the community seeks from its police service. I initiated this objective, independent examination because during my time as Commissioner I was at great pains to cement the links between the Met. and the capital . . . The results will not be known until next year, but I hope they will assist the Metropolitan Police in formulating its strategy for the rest of the decade and beyond.[11]

Having already argued that the Scarman Report implied that the police had been 'less than conscientious' in doing their job and therefore not receiving Scarman 'with complete enthusiasm', McNee put his trust in the PSI Report.

The Report provides a damning indictment of the police role in community relations. It shows clearly that the 'sniping of the critics' so despised by Sir David McNee was not only well founded but, if anything, has been markedly understated. The McNee-inspired 'objective' and 'independent' examination of the Metropolitan Police also exposes the extent to which Scarman's view of racism, to say nothing of sexism and classism, was blinkered. The account of the Metropolitan Police given in the Report is one of white, male, aspiring middle-class domination of blacks, women and the non-respectable working class. Each event and interview recorded in the participant observation study provides further evidence of the way in which police officers internalize and use images of the 'rough', the 'undeserving' and the 'inadequate'.

There is ample evidence that racism is institutional, pervasive and not confined to young, inexperienced officers. One detective chief inspector commented in an interview that 'Asians are incapable of telling the truth'; another found amusing 'extremely callous racialist jokes (including the one about renaming Deptford as Blackfriars)'; a commander in a 'sensitive area spontaneously spoke at length about the alien, unintelligible and threatening nature of the West Indian way of life'. The researchers endorse the findings of previous critical reports: black people are more likely to be stopped; the pervasive imagery in the force unquestioningly links blacks to crime; there is poor response to requests from Asians for action against racist attacks; demonstrations involving black people are more aggressively policed; in some cases racism may be the main cause of police aggression towards blacks. What is important is the way that police racism is *part of* a culture of values which revolves around white, masculine respectability. The PSI researchers show how the 'cult of masculinity' is constructed around heavy drinking and stories of fighting, violence and sexual conquest. Policewomen are purposefully excluded, humiliated and sexually harassed and are rejected 'as full members of the group or colleagues on an equal basis'.

The final victims of deep-seated prejudice are the 'slag' or the 'filth'. The Report states:

> A special conception of social class, mixed with an idea of conventional or proper behaviour, is just as important to police officers as racial or ethnic groups. In this scale the 'respectable' working class and the suburban middle class stand highest, while the 'underclass' of the poor and the rootless, together with groups regarded as deviant, such as homosexuals or hippies, stand lowest.[12]

The regular, institutionalized use of these images leads to their incorporation into the general ideology of police operations and practice. They are not, as Scarman would have us believe, the isolated actions of individual officers but form a central part of the political management of communities. This is the dominant ideology evident throughout police work. The PSI Report also concludes that police images of the people they deal with have a marked effect on their use of discretion, be it in arrest, detention, interrogation or prosecution. In other words, the prevailing view of 'niggers', 'coons', 'slags', 'filth', 'toe-rags' and so on is not only used to justify unjust treatment but also often violent and brutal responses. Again, the Report confirms what is well known in working-class communities: the police administer their own discretionary justice along with varying degrees of punishment.

The political management of neighbourhoods – the process by which state agencies assess, classify and define the destiny of working-class people – is based on perceptions of respectability, reputation and pathology. The PSI Report confirms these criteria as far as the present Metropolitan Police Force is concerned. The 'rough', the 'undeserving' and the 'dangerous' are well-established and lived constructions internalized within the policies and practices of the local state, the police, the magistracy and judiciary, the social services, the schools and the health services. In the wide-ranging, daily intervention of these agencies, ever defining and controlling the lives of individuals as clients, claimants, tenants or criminals, ideologies about personal inadequacy, cultural inferiority and neighbourhood reputation are central to the institutionalized practices of political management. These assumptions are all fed by their own academic, theoretical traditions producing specific programmes of treatment or remedy aimed at individuals or communities. While the consequences of this process are always serious, regardless of the agency involved, as Chapter 3 shows, the police have the added weight of their powers of arrest, detention, prosecution and, effectively, conviction. As was evident in the Merseyside case study and has been told in the PSI Report, police malpractice, verbal abuse, racial harassment and physical violence are all justified by presenting a context of violence, militancy and lawlessness within which the law has to be enforced. It is this dominant ideology, historically prevalent and deep within the police institution, which has been at the foundation of selective and discriminatory policing policies and practices.

Clearly crime has serious consequences for its victims. Violence, robbery and burglary cause immense suffering and personal trauma. On Merseyside's estates, for example, damage *is* inflicted *within* the working class. The consequences of anti-social behaviour and crime are as plain to see as the inhuman conditions dreamt up by the city's planners and architects and worsened by catastrophic government cuts and selective programmes of unemployment. Crime does fragment communities; it also reflects internal power relations. Violence against women, the victimization of old people and the climate of aggression which dominates so many social situations is primarily dictated, at the personal level, by male power and domination. It is a process which transcends class, culture and race boundaries. Black communities also experience the full force of white racism at both institutional and interpersonal levels. It is too easy to justify, or even to interpret, working-class crime solely as a form of resistance, however misdirected. Much of it is divisive and represents a real barrier to collective organization and political resistance.

Moreover, it is dangerous to consider crime only in terms of the terrain mapped out by the police. What is perceived as *the* crime problem – arriving on breakfast tables in the form of easily digestible percentages – is dictated largely by police priorities. The social and political consequences of crimes committed by the professionally respectable and economically powerful are minimized while the crimes of the poor are maximized. The political management of crime, the setting of boundaries for acceptable and non-acceptable behaviour, also operates at the level of negotiating after-hours drinking, street gambling and the handling of stolen goods. Police toleration of these and other 'offences' brings a reluctant acceptance by the public, not to be confused with consent, of their presence on the street. It is some measure of the hostility of the police towards inner-city black communities that such negotiations have never taken place.

6. Can you feel the force?

The public debate on the Scarman Report shifted the issue successfully from the power and autonomy of chief constables and the lack of political accountability to 'solutions' emphasizing the behaviour of individual police officers. What should have been a debate about power relations became diverted to 'specific problems' such as recruitment, training, management, race awareness and community consultation. Scarman's apparent lack of understanding of the crisis in police accountability was clear in his commitment to community liaison. The issue of consultation, however, along with the personalization of the race issue, also masked the legal and policy developments which have evolved since the new crisis in police accountability.

From 1980 to 1985, various structural proposals were put forward and led to certain developments. First there was a move towards strengthening the powers of police committees in the provinces (as exemplified in the 1980 Police Authorities (Powers) Bill proposed by Jack Straw MP and eventually adopted by the Labour Party) and the founding of an elected police authority for the GLC. The Bill was defeated. Second, the move, supported by ACPO and the Police Federation, towards consolidating the political autonomy of the police and extending police powers. The Thatcher administration responded with the Police and Criminal Evidence Bill. The Bill was redrafted several times and on 31 October 1984 became the Police and Criminal Evidence Act 1984 to be introduced in 1986. The first section of this chapter examines issues raised by the Straw Bill and the new Act.

The debate on the police also produced moves on policy. Firstly, there were calls for the centralization of the police by developing a national police force. Secondly, a determined move in inner-city areas and large towns towards community policing as proposed by Scarman. The second section of this chapter considers these two

policy moves and evaluates their significance as compared to other
not so visible, hard-line initiatives. The question of a national police
force is taken further in Chapter 7 where the policing of the coal
dispute is examined more thoroughly.

The tale of two Bills

The Straw Bill emerged from more general demands for 'greater
police accountability' to local government. As the confrontation
between the Merseyside Police Committee and its Chief Constable
became more severe, the Bill became the centre of fierce political
controversy. Although it failed in Parliament, the Bill's modest
proposals were endorsed by the 1981 Labour Conference.

The Bill was not an attempt to impose severe limitations on police
powers, nor did it propose new structures for political accountability. Its objective was to shift the balance of decision making
from chief constables to police authorities within the existing
'triangle of accountability'. It was drafted as an amendment to the
1964 Police Act which would 'establish and extend the powers and
duties of police authorities in respect of the operations and
organization of police forces'. Jack Straw argued:

> . . . police–public relations would be greatly improved if
> police authorities were given real powers to determine the
> *general* policing policies for their areas. To guard against the
> dangers of political interference in the proper discretion of
> chief officers in individual cases, two main safeguards could
> be provided. First, that where there is a fundamental
> disagreement of policy between a chief constable and his
> police authority the chief may activate a six-month 'cooling-
> off' period, that he may refer the dispute for final arbitration
> by the Home Secretary . . .

Straw's Bill aimed, as he put it, to place a 'firm hand' on police
policy and its priorities for enforcement. It was an attempt to give
the elected representatives of the local state a more direct say in the
formulation of police operational policy within their communities.
Straw noted that the main motivation behind the 1962 Royal
Commission's proposals had been to establish effective procedures
for consultation and accountability. His proposed reforms would

not encourage police committees 'to interfere in individual decisions on prosecutions, or to sit in permanent session to decide on what response the police should make to 999 calls'. Rather, his aim was to establish a clear framework within which elected councillors, as the police committee, would have a 'say in the *general* policies of their areas'. Police committees would become more involved in appointing senior officers, would have access to regular reports on their forces from the Inspectors of Constabulary and would possess more formal powers to initiate complaints against chief constables.

A main plank in the Straw Bill was the requirement on chief constables to submit a proposed programme of policy recommendations every year to the police committees. This would be accepted or rejected, in full or in part, by the committee. Disputes between chief constables and police committees would be referred to the Home Secretary for arbitration. This proposed shift in the balance of decision making was in line with the idea of 'shared responsibility' proposed by Margaret Simey. Straw's intention to pin down chief constables and police committees to an agreed programme would enable local councillors to make chief constables accountable for the generally agreed and shared guiding principles for the policing of their areas.

The reaction to the Straw proposals and the mounting public concern over political accountability drew a mixed response from the police. The concept of direct community consultation over local police strategies was already established as a cornerstone of Alderson's community policing programme throughout Devon and Cornwall. The then Assistant Chief Constable of Nottingham, Geoffrey Dear, echoed Alderson's sentiments in an article published during 1980. He argued that 'the public at large should be *counselled* as to their views on the evolvement of any list of priorities'. This was 'entirely logical . . . if limited and valuable resources are to be funded by public money and expended in the public good'.[2] As with the Alderson initiative, Dear insisted that this process of community consultation would not determine or alter the role of police authorities; nor would it undermine or change the powers of the chief constable. He concluded:

Such a list [of priorities] would *necessarily* be loosely formulated, and the *autonomy* of the chief police officers should remain unaltered, but it must be right that society

should be consulted concerning the areas of work in which
the police and other agencies are to be largely concentrated,
and asked which areas the *public can assist themselves*, albeit
with professional help and advice. (Emphasis added)

Here is a clear admission that chief officers are, and should remain,
autonomous of the democratic process. Dear's remarks show that
the intention of consultation was limited. There was no provision
for the extension of powers to police authorities or local communities. Consultation did not mean control.

As we shall see later, Alderson's model of community consultation, within a framework of community policing, emerged at this
time as a significant formula in an attempt to establish and claim
'policing by consent'. In 1982 the Merseyside Working Group on
Police-Community Relations echoed the move towards community
consultation centres. This recommendation was adopted by both
the Merseyside Police Committee and its Chief Constable.
Scarman's endorsement of community consultation clearly influenced its broader adoption. Each of these programmes also reflects
Alderson's programme for inter-agency co-operation and exchange
of information about specific individuals, families or communities.

Other influential police sources based their opposition to the
Straw Bill on the issue of political control. James Anderton, Chief
Constable of Greater Manchester, had no illusions as to the main
thrust of Straw's 'quite extraordinary Bill'. He commented:

In essence . . . the Bill seeks to limit the powers of chief
constables by *forcing* them, as a matter of law, to *co-operate*
with police authorities where presently the issues *are left to
the good sense and professional understanding of those concerned*
. . . Equally incredible is the proposition that police
committees should have the statutory right of *involvement* in
the critical analysis of police operational problems and a *real
say* in the general deployment of police resources, even to
the extent of issuing directions to the chief constable.[3]
(Emphasis added)

Anderton's use of the terms 'co-operation', 'involvement' and
'real say' are here stressed to show that the Bill was not in fact about
making the police more politically accountable, but was only a

vehicle for greater political control of chief officers. A system based on 'good sense and professional understanding' (what Simey referred to as a 'gentleman's agreement') would undermine and deny 'the individual and professional integrity of chief constables'. Anderton's position endorses the political autonomy of chief constables and suggests that their professional judgement is sufficient to justify and maintain that autonomy. According to Anderton, the hands of chief constables would have been firmly tied under the Straw legislation. He concluded that police critics had two main objectives:

> The political power to control and direct the day-to-day operations of the police with all that implies, and the power to prevent a chief constable from speaking freely in public on matters germane to his duties.

At the centre of Anderton's view of things is his firm belief that the Bill aimed to remove full operational control of the police from chief constables and to place it in the hands of elected, lay representatives. In his eyes greater political accountability is a mask for total political control. The logical conclusion of this view – political control of the police – is the perceived threat which apparently unites senior police officers. Sir Robert Mark, former Commissioner of the Metropolitan Police, described these developments as 'the thin edge of subversion of the operational independence of the police'.[4] Using the issue of party political control, he stated:

> . . . the operational control of the police should never become the responsibility of *one or other* political party . . . The accountability of the police to democratically constituted authorities ultimately controlled by Parliament itself is their strongest guarantee of support, because it ensures that they reflect the will of the people as a whole, and not just the government in power.

Mark paid little attention to the relationship of UK democracy to the party system or to the issue of how Parliament can be more representative of 'the people as a whole' than local government. This line of argument insists that the controversies on political accountability are in fact about the boundaries of political control.

Yet Mark reaffirms his commitment to police accountability to 'democratically constituted authorities'. Other senior police officers, as we have seen from the comments of Alderson and Dear, feel that consensus policing can only be reached by closer involvement of the police in community life, interagency co-operation and regular community consultation. This does not necessarily constitute an alternative position on accountability, rather it represents a different strategy for police involvement in communities. For they too maintain that the autonomy of the police in establishing operational policies and enforcement priorities needs to be defended from any further encroachment via legislation.

Sir David McNee, Mark's successor, expressed few doubts about 'those who have vested interest in undermining our authority and seeking to destroy our tradition of policing by consent'. He argued that the subversion of the authority of the police was not the prerogative of 'the obvious extremist':

> . . . there are those with apparent good intent who by
> injudicious criticism undermine the maintenance of the law.
> I am currently facing criticism from certain quarters, for
> example, for the priority my officers give to the prevention
> of street crime and burglary. It is particularly irritating
> when the criticism comes from church leaders who should
> be concerned more with the spiritual role, and from certain
> politicians who perhaps ought to concentrate more on the
> eradication of inner-city deprivation.[5]

Presumably the policies defended here by McNee were those of saturation policing, SUS and 'stop and search' – all of which had drawn informed criticism and public statements of concern from church leaders and politicians. His contention that these policies and their consequences should be outside the concerns of the spiritual wellbeing and political interests of communities was itself an indication of where he set the boundaries to the politics of police work. In his much publicized and apparently highly lucrative 'retirement articles' for the *Sunday Mirror*, McNee commented that such is the 'complexity of police work today' that the police 'not only face the criminal, but also the political extremist who fastens onto any headline–making issue in order to achieve *power*'.[6] In his comments on Grunwick, McNee again linked 'extremism' to middle-of-the-road politics:

> I didn't bother with the nonsensical sayings of Arthur
> Scargill at Grunwick. But I did wonder at the presence on
> the picket line of a number of Members of Parliament, of
> both the Left and the Right. For they were the opinion
> makers whose involvement ensured that the media had to be
> on the scene – thereby providing the extremists with the
> publicity they badly craved . . . For the presence of such
> people is taken by extremists as an endorsement of violent
> confrontation.

In his criticism of these 'naive or politically opportunist' MPs, it
seemed that it was McNee himself who considered their presence at
Grunwick as an 'endorsement of violent confrontation'. Nowhere
did he evaluate the serious criticisms of police violence at Grunwick
which came from many quarters. Politicians who responded to this
public concern and went to 'see for themselves' have since found
their attendance portrayed as nothing more than an endorsement of
extremism. McNee failed to appreciate that it is a legitimate
function of elected politicians to concern themselves with issues
such as the policing of industrial conflict or inner-city communities.
For example, it was precisely the issue of inner-city deprivation
which lay behind the Merseyside Police Committee's criticism of
police operations in Toxteth.

Confrontation over what constitutes police accountability, where
the boundaries of political control are to be set and how far elected
politicians should intervene in negotiating a programme of priorities
for law enforcement in their communities, has become a central
issue in the policing of the 1980s. Straw's attempt to get a firm hand
on the police drew the response from the police that it would be a
strangler's grip. Consequently, all attempts by individual police
committees to intervene, even retrospectively, in policy matters
have been resisted by senior officers. Not only did the resistance to
calls for 'greater accountability' unite senior officers, also it united
police senior management and the Police Federation.

This united front has described the demand for greater accountability in extremist, subversionary, totalitarian images. The Straw
Bill was presented as the thin end of the wedge: a Bill designed to
undermine the professional integrity of the police and abolish their

operational independence. The imagery used had a profound effect on the debate concerning accountability and contributed to the rejection of the Bill. While the debate was in process, however, another quite different Police Bill was being drafted. This was the government-backed Police and Criminal Evidence Bill, first published in December 1982 and revised after the re-election of the Tories in June 1983. It owes much to the evidence of Sir David McNee to the 1980 Royal Commission on Criminal Procedure; it effectively extends police powers and consolidates police autonomy.

McNee's recommendations were far-reaching. They included the removal of restrictions on powers of search, the power to stop and search vehicles and their occupants on police authority alone, compulsory fingerprinting on the authority of a judge, and the full disclosure of personal bank accounts on magistrates' authority. Powers of arrest would become statutory and detention would be possible early in an investigation with the objective of 'obtaining of *prima facie* proof'. The right to detain for questioning without charge would be extended to 72 hours on the authority of a magistrate. The 'right to silence' would be withdrawn – silence would be used to indicate a person's implication or direct involvement in an offence. In assessing the significance of McNee's recommendations, one commentator said at the time:

> McNee's proposals have dominated public perception of the
> work of the Royal Commission. They have strongly
> influenced the proposals emerging from the rest of the
> police. They are undoubtedly the most influential set of
> recommendations received by the Commission, and the
> most detailed manifesto of police intentions in the exercise
> of their principal task: the enforcement of criminal law.[7]

When the Police Bill eventually emerged the stamp of the former Commissioner was evident throughout its content. The police were to be given new national powers to stop and search, set up roadblocks and make arrests. Stop and search powers were to be extended to any situation where the police had 'reasonable suspicion' that individuals or vehicles might be carrying stolen goods, 'offensive weapons' or any articles which could be used in a burglary or theft. What constituted an offensive weapon or qualified as an article potentially for use in theft remained open to police interpretation and discretion. The police would be obliged to identify themselves and provide reasons for searching but there were no sanctions proposed for dealing with officers who broke the rules. Yet the Royal Commission had warned that 'without stringent controls . . . abuse is possible'.

The Royal Commission had also warned that roadblocks should be used to seal off an area only when a particularly grave offence had been committed or when a 'dangerous person' was known to be at large in an area. In such cases the Royal Commission recommended that authorization for roadblocks should be given only by the chief constable or assistant chief constable and then only for a restricted period. The Bill, however, empowered superintendents to authorize roadblocks for up to seven days on the grounds that a 'serious arrestable offence is *likely* to be committed'. The police were to use their discretion to make their judgements bearing in mind the 'pattern of crime' in a given area.

The Bill proposed the extension of police powers, supported by a magistrate's warrant, to search premises where the owner or occupier was *not* under suspicion but where there might be evidence of a 'serious arrestable offence'. Following an arrest, subsequent entry to the premises concerned would be at the discretion of the police. The police would have the powers to search the premises. Thus they could enter premises and, after gaining access, arrest people for offences unrelated to the reason given for entry. Again it is important to note that the Royal Commission considered that this should be a 'last resort' power to be granted in 'exceptional circumstances and in respect of grave offences' and then granted only on the authorization of a circuit judge. The Bill was in fact quite different once drafted – providing for general searches relating to serious, arrestable offences on the authorization of a magistrate alone.

The Bill also proposed the extension of powers of arrest for non-imprisonable offences, empowering the police to make arrests in order to prevent people from doing harm to themselves, or where they believe that a person has given false particulars. Other categories included 'affront to public decency', the obstruction of a highway or where property *might be* damaged. Again there was no clear sanction for wrongful arrest and the ambiguity of the categories presented the police with such broad discretion that unlawful arrest would be difficult to establish.

The Bill proposed that the police should be given the power to arrest and detain where there were 'reasonable grounds for believing that detention without charge is necessary to secure or preserve evidence' or where such evidence might be obtained through questioning. It would allow the police to detain a person for 36 hours on their own authority and up to 60 hours with a magistrate's authorization. Powers to obtain fingerprints, to conduct intimate body searches or to take intimate body samples, using force if necessary, were also provided for in the Bill. There was no right of access to a solicitor, except after 36 hours. The police would be able to waive detainees' rights concerning the grounds and conditions of detention if, in their judgement, it was not convenient to interrupt the questioning. What appeared in the Bill as 'rights' of detainees were no more than discretionary guidelines for the first 36 hours of detention.

The Police Bill drew considerable opposition, particularly from the legal and medical professions and the churches. Some of the criticisms, especially those relating to confidential records and body searches, were amended at the committee stage of the Bill. The second Thatcher government, with Leon Brittan now Home Secretary, introduced a revised Bill in October 1983. The Act was finally passed a year later. In line with the criticisms received from the British Medical Association, the use of intimate body searches without a suspect's consent was rejected. The police retain this power, however, if they have 'reason to believe' that a suspect is concealing a weapon which could be used on themselves or on others. Superintendents will be able to authorize officers to make these searches. It is a considerable discretionary power. Following criticisms from the Law Society over what constitutes a 'serious arrestable offence', the Home Office tightened the definition. The list of such offences is given in Chapter 3. Finally, the Home Office attempted to reassure those who have criticized the proposed extension of police powers by arguing that the safeguards given to suspects will be strengthened.

Despite some significant changes and compromises, the revised Police and Criminal Evidence Act has retained the central themes of its predecessor. It will introduce an 'independent' police complaints authority. The authority will be empowered to supervise the investigation of complaints against officers and will replace the Police Complaints Board in disciplinary matters. It will vet officers appointed to an investigation, give instructions to investigating officers, supervise all complaints relating to death or serious injury and any cases deemed 'in the public interest', particularly corruption and police assault. Through its supervisory role the new authority will assess the thoroughness, speed and efficiency of the investigation and handling of cases by the police. Furthermore, the disciplinary authority will be empowered to bring proceedings against officers regardless of the DPP's decision concerning prosecution. The Home Secretary also announced six experimental programmes to tape-record police interviews of suspects at police stations. Transcripts of interviews will be made available to defence counsel and, in the case of a dispute over content, the tapes will be used in court.

The most controversial issues raised by the first Bill have remained with only minor modifications. The extension to all forces of stop and search powers is retained. The police will be expected to keep detailed records of searches, and anyone searched by the police will be entitled to a written explanation of why he or she was searched. From the mass of evidence available from those areas where stop and search is already used, it is clear that the extension of this power will bring further difficulties in police-community relations. The selective use of stop and search powers, directed particularly and most regularly against black people, is almost impossible to check. The police justify their actions in each case on the grounds of 'reasonable suspicion'. They see a particular relationship between 'types of crime' and 'types of individuals' or 'communities' – a picture which binds different crimes to various stereotyped criminals – and out of this construct their boundaries of 'reasonable suspicion'. The stereotype fits the crime and, given this construction, all stereotypes must be under suspicion, even if no specific crime has been committed. It is this 'inevitable logic' which has enabled the police to use, arbitrarily and consistently, SUS, stop and search and swamp tactics against black people. The claim that a written justification for a personal stop and search will make the police more accountable or more hesitant in their day-to-day practices is doubtful when set against the history of police interventions in black communities.

The issue of discretion dominates the phrasing of the Act and will continue to dominate the use and abuse of police powers. For example, the use of roadblocks to seal off areas or communities on the grounds that an offence is 'likely' to be committed leaves the police free to use roadblocks as they feel appropriate. This merely affirmed the use of roadblocks during the coal dispute. The checks on the powers of search in the form of magistrates' warrants for general searches, or judges' warrants for access to confidential records, will be dispensed with if it is police opinion that important evidence might be removed or be at risk. While random searches, so-called 'fishing expeditions', will be unlawful and apparently at an end, the police can use any evidence they find, providing the initial search is lawful. The extension of the powers of arrest, as shown in Chapter 3, highlights the permissiveness of discretion. If a person suspected of a minor offence is thought to have given false or dubious personal details he or she will be liable to arrest. The police will be able to make arrests when there could be injury to people or property, where there is a danger of a highway being obstructed or where there is an 'affront to public decency'. The use of these categories is left to the momentary responses of individual officers. The abuse of these new powers will be virtually impossible to control. That injuries *might* result from particular actions, that public decency – whatever that is – has been affronted, that a highway might be obstructed are variations on the same theme. They are about the assessment of likelihood, as in 'likely to cause a breach of the peace', and are clearly permissive – therefore easily abused – powers. The shooting of Steven Waldorf and the subsequent trial of two police officers emphasized, in a most dramatic way, that as long as it is reasonable to believe that the police have acted in good faith then the public must bear the brunt of any mistakes. The distinction between an 'honest mistake' and 'deliberate abuse' will be very difficult to draw.

Prior to the passing of the Act, as McNee readily admitted, the treatment of people detained for questioning in police custody gave serious cause for concern. The use of force, usually claimed by the police as 'reasonable' in order to 'restrain' a difficult person, was the focus of a good deal of controversy. The deaths of people like Jimmy Kelly on Merseyside and James Davey in the West Midlands raised serious questions about police procedures in making arrests and how far the public is protected against excessive force. Mass arrests in North Wales in 1980 relating to arson campaigns directed against second-home ownership in the country drew further serious criticism. People were taken from their beds during the night or snatched from the street and then held for several days. With no access granted to lawyers and no information given to friends and relatives concerning their whereabouts, those arrested virtually disappeared for several days. Eventually they were returned to their homes without being charged. They had been subjected to searching and very personal interrogation without legal advice or representation. Because of the nature of the resulting campaign the cases received a good deal of well-informed publicity.

The abuse of rights in arrest and detention concerns not only the occasional serious case of assault or brutality or the occasional trawl of 'political activists'. Serious though these cases are, they can be dismissed as aberrations in an otherwise smooth-running, protective system. However, while most people are released from questioning within a few hours or on the same day, it is not unusual for suspects to be questioned for days without access to a solicitor or to relatives and friends. The 'safeguards' of Judges' Rules are ignored as a matter of course and the protection afforded by habeas corpus is rarely used. As McNee's evidence to the Royal Commission indicated, these practices – irregular but not illegal – have become institutionalized.

The Police Act has confirmed this process of institutionalization. The powers given to the police to hold suspects up to 24 hours in ordinary cases and up to 96 hours with a magistrate's approval after the first 36 hours in serious cases, set the seal of legality on what until now have constituted abuses of powers. Defenders of the Act pointed to the 60-plus pages which constitute the new code of practice, nominally providing a detained person with protection during detention and questioning. The code provides the right to a record of all that happens while in custody. This includes information concerning rights, access to a solicitor, rest periods and other specific issues such as the rights of householders concerning search. While the code binds the police, sanctions for breaking the code are administered internally through disciplinary proceedings. Again, discretion is the crucial issue. It is left to the police to decide on the validity of complaints and on the operation of the code. For example, the so-called 'absolute' right to a solicitor obtains in all but the most serious cases. Who draws the line between 'less serious' and 'most serious' and the criteria used to inform their judgement is a crucial discretionary power. Needless to say, it will lie with the police and the ever-present notion of being 'reasonable'.

National structures and community strategies

The discussion of police accountability in Chapter 3 argued that the 1964 Police Act has given chief constables political autonomy both in the construction of overall operational policy and in the setting of priorities for law enforcement. This has been consolidated further since the 1964 Act by a substantial reduction in the number of police forces, bringing an equivalent reduction in the number of chief constables. The fewer the number of chief constables, the more centralized their influence. They operate, therefore, with greater authority and 'speak' for a greater geographical area. ACPO, the formal body of chief constables' opinion, has become a tightly knit forum. Its influence with governments, as E.P. Thompson has noted, fundamentally undermines the democratic process.[8] Persistent challenges to the political autonomy of chief constables, mainly as a result of police responses to the 'riots', have produced some significant reactions. James Anderton's comments on p. 85 show that in his view awkward questions from his police committee indicate an attempt to subvert the operations of the police. His answer to awkward questions appears to be to abandon the premise of democratic control and do away with the questioner – the abolition of the police authority.

While the debates over the political control of the police and the extension of police powers have remained within the confines of existing structural arrangements, the Anderton response to the confrontations between police authorities and their chief constables shows a quite different emphasis. This is seen in the renewed call for structural change in the form of a centralized, national police force. Another apparently different response has been a more general commitment – particularly after the Scarman Report – to community–based strategies of police work. Here the problem is located *not* at the level of operational policy decisions but in the personal relations and daily contact between the police and local communities. The contrast between these two positions, at least on the surface, is more marked.

A move towards consolidating the autonomy of chief constables seemed inevitable. James Anderton has argued for a further reduction in the number of chief constables to a regional organization of about ten forces. This would provide a 'cabal' of chief constables, a kind of inner cabinet for the nation's policing, and would centralize operations even further. In this structure regional boards could replace locally based police committees. Meanwhile, even the more traditional biographers of the police, such as Critchley, consider that police accountability was effectively eroded through the last round of reductions in the number of forces. Anderton and others argue that further reductions would bring economies of scale, greater efficiency and a cutback in diversification of resources. The new organization would leave the real professionals to make informed decisions and diminish the effectiveness of ill-informed lay-people.

This line of reasoning has been taken a stage further by Eric St Johnstone, a former Inspector of Constabulary, in a discussion of situations 'where a police authority and its chief constable do not see eye to eye'. He commented:

> If a provincial police committee has the same views as the members of the unofficial committee of the GLC (i.e. that the Special Branch and the Special Patrol Group should be abolished against the wishes of the chief constable), a local constitutional crisis of considerable magnitude could arise. This is becoming more likely as *the calibre of views* of an increasing number of members of local authorities change. In the past there has been a community of interest and mutual respect between the chief constable and the police committee. This is in danger of breaking down. The question has to be asked whether the public would now be better served by having a national police force divorced from local control.[9] (Emphasis added)

St Johnstone argued that the events of the previous two years had brought a shift in police opinion towards a national police force. The main position is clear and echoes Anderton's statements, namely that democracy is acceptable as long as the elected representatives are submissive and compliant. As soon as the first murmurings of dissent are heard, the first chief constable challenged, then 'mutual respect' is broken and the 'good old days' of private gentlemen's agreements have passed. What we have heard in the police committee chambers on Merseyside and in Greater Manchester have not been the questioning voices of democracy but councillors of a quite different 'calibre' with quite different 'views'. The assumption is again one of subversion.

The lobby for a national police force has made, as we have seen, the not unreasonable claim that it could produce greater efficiency and consistency via cost efficiency and common policies, priorities and practices. It is the logical conclusion to calls for a further reduction in the number of forces, regionalization and a lessening of local authority involvement. The centralized framework has already been affirmed by ACPO. Using disputes about accountability as a justification for nationalizing the police is, however, a new departure. St Johnstone concludes that the chief constable 'is only answerable to the laws of this country', but

> Perhaps the time has come when he should be *directly*
> answerable to Parliament. It is only reasonable that if the
> Home Secretary is to carry responsibility for law and order
> in this country then he should have full powers to direct and
> control.

This last phrase sounds warning bells for chief officers. The 'full powers' of direction and control, i.e. political control, would not leave chief constables 'answerable to Parliament' but to the government of the day. Under this proposal chief constables would be directed and controlled not only by the law but by the Home Secretary. This they find unacceptable. More acceptable to chief constables is the notion of community policing. At first sight it moves the emphasis away from structural changes within a 'national' force to questions of strategy at a 'local', community-interventionist level. This framework would seem to unite the parties, the police and many of their critics. Operationally, however, community policing is not all that it seems.

For John Alderson, community policing provided a radical alternative to 'fire-brigade' responses to incidents which, he argued, now dominated police operations.[10] His reorganization of the Devon and Cornwall force emphasized community-based policing: more direct involvement by the police in the day-to-day affairs of the community and the police more personally visible. By putting the police back into the community and giving individual officers a regular beat, the community would come to know 'their' officers. This would bring mutual trust and friendship. The police needed to show greater interest in the daily affairs of people (the police officer as social worker) and also to become more directly concerned with the formal workings of neighbourhoods. They needed to build strong relationships with other key workers in the community – to liaise with youth workers, community service workers and others committed to developing the quality of life in the community. Helping in youth clubs and organizing social activities were two examples of such community work.

The idea of shared responsibility for the social life of the community also appeared in Alderson's plan for inter-agency co-operation. Here he proposed that all agencies involved in the 'care' and servicing of communities should come together more formally in a joint programme. The collective strength of the professional presence in a community could be used to the benefit of any individuals, families or groups with particular 'problems'. Social workers, doctors, priests, community workers, teachers, academics, voluntary organizations and other 'specialists' would meet together with the police in order to identify problems in the community and, through shared information and collective enterprise, would respond in the best interests of the clients. The programme would rely on a frank and open relationship between agencies. The 'Community Workers' Group' set up in Skelmersdale New Town in the late seventies is an example of an inter-agency group which focused its attention on interventionist strategies in the community. Its members came from a whole range of professional agencies and it dealt with often very specific issues and 'problems'. The police officer who attended this group rarely contributed to the discussion. Specific cases were discussed and no check was kept on how that information, often of a confidential nature, was interpreted and used by the police.

While co-operation between agencies is presented as a genuine attempt to understand and work with the 'problems' of a community, it clearly has a great potential for surveillance. How far the confidentiality of the professional-client relationship can be penetrated by well-intentioned 'support' programmes is left to the discretion and mutual trust of the workers involved. In the Skelmersdale group it was clear that information which would have been closely guarded by workers in any formal approach by the police was casually offered in the course of discussion at group meetings. There was no procedure for making this self-appointed group accountable for its information sharing or decisions. This raises the issue of the final part of Alderson's strategy: that of community consultation.

Alderson's programme, published in 1980, challenged an 'authoritarian' style of policing by suggesting that 'a partnership between police and public' should be forged and promising 'ordinary people a say in the complex problems of law and order'.[11] The 'say' was the opportunity to meet with the police at public meetings and discuss priorities for policing in their neighbourhood. People could also make comments on the efficiency and style of existing policies and practices. This forum was to be supported by a policy of increased consultation at a personal level. The move towards public meetings and consultation 'clinics' has, however, left the responsibility for participation with the local community. It assumes that if people do *not* use the machinery of consultation, their consent can be taken for granted. There is no consideration that people might lack the confidence to make complaints or be intimidated by the procedure. Yet this commitment to community consultation has been used as an indication that the police are becoming more in tune with local communities, more responsive to the demands of their inhabitants and, therefore, more accountable to the people. Consultation, however, should not be confused with accountability. The process of community consultation gives no community access to the procedures of accountability. People can state their dissatisfaction with the police and they can offer advice, but the police are under no obligation to do what they ask. A strategy for closer involvement by the community in the policing of their streets is no more than an elaborate exercise in public relations.

Alderson's programme was no doubt intended as an antidote to the larger forces whose reactive style had the finesse of a sledgehammer. But it was never meant as a total replacement. The programme stated:

> Communal policing offers an alternative strategy to the power solution of ever-bigger police batallions, increased dependence on technology and undue reliance on the system of criminal justice as a preventive force . . . it provides a *complementary element* in a *total police strategy* which includes preventive patrols, incident cars, task forces and criminal investigation. (Emphasis added)

So, preventive community policing was not a radical alternative to the reactive sledgehammer of the large-scale forces. After coming under some fire from his senior colleagues and following several articles which cast him in the 'radical alternative' mould, Alderson stated clearly in a letter to *New Society* that community policing should be part of a police strategy which would include more forceful operational tactics.

Until the uprisings of 1980–1 and the Scarman Report, there was only limited support within the police for Alderson's strategies. Community policing was a 'soft alternative' in situations which demanded 'hard-line' responses. Throughout the police the general response was that in towns and cities, the identified 'centres of crime and violence', the community-based approach would not work. Alderson was depicted as a naive idealist operating in a cosy, sleepy backwater. Officers on the beat argued that there was no way into the trust of communities which had a deep, if not pathological, hatred of the police.

While police attitudes remained unchanged after the disturbances, wider pressures on them to develop a closer and more tolerant relationship with inner-city communities grew. As the Merseyside case study indicates, Alderson's ideas informed the political debate and were endorsed by the Police Committee. This brought community consultation and the introduction of 'local patrols'. Scarman provided the most influential pressure towards community-based programmes. His report on the Brixton disorders openly criticized the saturation tactics that had been used and the racism of young officers. It called for greater police familiarity with communities and their needs, for better training, for the dismissal of racist officers and for closer relationships between agencies. Scarman endorsed the fundamental principles of community policing.

After Scarman's criticisms of the Metropolitan Police other forces were quick to defend their approach as 'community based'. Almost all forces have well-established programmes of specialist interventions in local neighbourhoods. These include 'community relations' officers, whose work is to meet the 'problems' posed by 'coloured communities'.[12] By 1976, 29 of the 43 police forces in England and Wales were doing specialist work in 'community relations', and 17 had specialist departments. Often seen within the forces as a 'soft option' and not 'real police work', community relations officers work within a sceptical, if not hostile, atmosphere. The general framework was one in which black communities were targeted as '*the* problem'. While community relations police thought they were sympathetic towards black communities – in comparison to other specialized units such as the Special Patrol Group – they never considered that the real problem might be white racism and its institutionalization.

Another identifiable group targeted for special 'community-based' attention was youth. The first juvenile liaison scheme was established in Liverpool as early as 1949 in order to preempt juvenile crime. Within three years it was a department in Liverpool's Crime Prevention Branch and became the model adopted by the Home Office in advising all other forces. This work laid the base for the first community-policing programme, initiated in 1956 by David Gray in Greenock. The embryo of Alderson's work is easy to identify in the Greenock initiative – close liaison with other local government agencies and a regular commitment to programmes of youth work has become the basis of police intervention with local youth. From these foundations regular juvenile liaison work has become a central focus of preventive policing and has involved close work with schools, youth clubs, probation officers and education welfare.

Police work in schools highlights one of the most controversial aspects of interventionist programmes. It has gained considerable support from forces since the mid-seventies, by which time several forces had seconded police officers with sole responsibility for working in schools. Other forces made beat officers responsible for this as part of their regular duties. In Devon and Cornwall a joint scheme between police and the local education authority was developed; in North Wales officers were based at the local education offices. In 1980 a police officer in Hampshire was appointed full time to a 'large and troublesome comprehensive' and a year later four officers joined the staff of a Durham comprehensive. The school timetable included lessons on the police role in the community, on the social costs of crime and on vandalism.[13] By the following January the scheme was extended to other schools in Durham. The main focus of the scheme was pupils between 11 and 13 – older pupils were considered to be already hardened in their views. The meaning of 'preventive' was quite clear: young children were asked to pass information to the police concerning vandalism, theft or anything suspicious.[14] In Devon and Cornwall school intervention developed to the point of having 24 full-time officers covering the 1,000 or so schools in the authority. A 'moral education adviser' was appointed jointly by the police and the education authority.[15] The close involvement of the police with young people in schools raises fundamental questions about the confidentiality of information held by teachers about young people and their families. And what about pupils being encouraged to spy on each other and 'grass' to the police?

Finally, contradictory behaviour by 'community' and patrol police is highlighted by the following examples. In 1981, in response to a playground incident at Archway School, North London, the police sent out six cars and a helicopter. According to pupils black children were assaulted by the police and racist abuse, such as 'black bastard' and 'nigger lover', was used. The police commented that this was 'the usual standard sort of propaganda about police going in with big boots on the kids. We did not go in with big boots. We responded as we should have responded . . . the response was excellent'.[16] The school did not agree and the police-schools programme at the school was terminated.

In 1983 a head teacher at a large comprehensive in Milton Keynes confirmed the estrangement that often exists between police-school liaison officers and the patrol police. A young pupil who had stolen a staff member's cheque card was handcuffed by the police in the head teacher's office. The head's protest was greeted with an offhand response. It was made clear to him that once he had brought the police onto the school premises in response to an offence he had no effective control over the way in which they handled the situation. He cited other examples of other 'over-the-top' reactions which included the driving of a patrol car at speed in the school grounds. In his opinion, any 'trust' between the police and his pupils, built over time by school-police liaison, was lost in a few minutes by officers who in practice had defeated the whole object of classroom theorizing and promises.[17]

The real intention of much police-school liaison is underlined by an officer's account from experience in the Lothian and Borders Police:

> We go down to the schools a lot. You get a hell of a lot of information from the kids. They get wise to us once they're

about seven or eight, but they still like to boast about what their big brothers or their dads have been up to so we get a lot off the teachers.[18]

The gathering of information without any check on how it may be used, the engineering and structuring of the notion of 'policing by consent' and the direct involvement of young pupils in policing their friends and neighbours are all examples of what community-policing initiatives mean in practice. They are delivered and publicized with the smiling goodwill of liberal responses to serious problems. The ethics are dubious, to say the least. As Scarman noted:

> Police assistance in the education of children in the
> fundamentals of an ordered society can, however, be of great
> value . . . Obviously there are limits to the proper activities
> of the police in schools – it would be wholly inappropriate,
> for example, for police officers routinely to enter school
> premises in order to question children about suspected
> offences.[19]

The problem with the relationship between the police and schools, however, is how the line is drawn over questioning and information gathering. The 'programmes' of police intervention in schools are presented as being progressive and useful to the creation of good relations. On Merseyside in 1979, for example, the Chief Constable wrote to all schools in the area to launch a school-centred scheme under the heading of 'Into the Eighties with Pride'. His statement stressed the laudable intentions of co-operation and close working relations. Some teachers interviewed at the time, however, expressed concern at police access to schools and at the possibility of confidentiality being breached. Their main concern was that there were no effective checks on police activity in schools.

This implicit lack of trust in police intentions has been reinforced by police statements which suggest that community-policing initiatives are underpinned by other motives. The present Commissioner of the Metropolitan Police, Sir Kenneth Newman, has stated the need to develop 'new strategies for dealing with inner-city problems' through the co-operation of 'all agencies involved in *social control*'.[20] Inter-agency co-operation is here described in terms of a controlling function. And the community-policing 'strategy' as adopted consistently reflects Newman's identification with social control. The job specification for community police officers in the Lothian and Borders Police, for example, states that they should

> Secure the services of at least one observer in every street, not a paid professional informant, but someone who knows the inhabitants and is inquisitive enough to find out what is going on and who is willing to pass such information gained.[21]

The cultivation of community spies lists shopkeepers, tradespeople and garage staff, and rates high on the assessment of the 'effectiveness' of police officers. This information is fed to the local force collator's office for distribution. The office is in the main area police station and the collator is a police officer. Just what is contained in collators' reports is not clear. However, in 1982 a report from the Skelmersdale collator's office came to light. As Skelmersdale New Town was selected as a special area for testing out community-policing strategies, the collator's report, dated Tuesday 14 September 1982, is of special interest. It is headed Bulletin 60/82 which suggests that by mid-September in one year there had been 60 such bulletins. On Bulletin 60 there are nine typed entries from police officers in Skelmersdale, Ormskirk and surrounding districts, and two photographs. A typical entry, alongside a photograph of a black man, reads as follows:

> The Right Man for the Job.
> . . . [name] . . . [damage] of . . . [address] – known affectionately to his CB mates as 'Tonka Toy' . . . paid another return visit to our fair division at 3.30 a.m. on Friday 10.9. 82 when he was stopped/checked in his nifty yellow Capri CTB 498J . . . Gracefully reclining in the passenger seat was none other than school breaker and suspected druggie . . .[name] . . .[wounding, burglary, theft, damage] of . . . [address], whose unforgettable features are pictured left. . . .[name] augments his hard-earned dole money by working on the door at [night club] keeping out other undesirables. [name] and [name] are well acquainted

with the finer points of our Division and are worth every stop/check they can get.

All the accounts in this report reflect this cynical attitude. Another person was 'checked' in the early hours 'wearily dragging his feet . . . carrying all of his personal belongings in a plastic carrier bag'. It continues:

> Apparently, big sister had cracked him over the head with a bottle of orange squash and given him his marching orders from the family mansion at . . . [address] . . . [name] seemed at a loss to know where he would be living for the next fortnight but said that he was due to be given the tenancy of a flat at . . . [address]. The next question is, of course, how . . . [name] proposes to furnish his new abode but no doubt his form for theft and handling (as well as assault) should land him in good stead.

Entries include personal details of people stopped, checked or thought to be in the area. Previous convictions are given as a matter of course but casual and often defamatory comments about the life style, appearance or alleged activities of individuals are common. People, apparently without any criminal record, are mentioned simply because they associated with 'known' faces. Following an account of a Mercedes being found in a respectable area in which the owner had claimed that he had broken down and left the car, the report continued:

> The police at Crosby have their own theory, however, as . . . [name] has the deplorable habit of leaving vehicles in unusual places and the Mercedes may have been left there for the benefit of someone else. . . . [name] is apparently something in the motor trade and has previous for deception and theft of a motor vehicle . . . and anyone using one of his cars should be worth a stop/search.

A final entry, under the heading of 'Your everywish', states that the 'ever-fortunate residents of the Beaconsview Old People's Home . . . are currently benefitting from the attentions of . . . [name] who is taking part in the Hindley Borstal's Community Scheme'. This concludes a series of negative comments about individuals, the community and, in the last example, the very kind of community initiative to which the police claim they are committed.

The use of the collator's office to disseminate all kinds of information gathered from a range of often unnamed sources raises the question of the keeping of non-criminal records. For years the police have reassured critics that they do not keep records on people who have not been convicted of crimes. Yet under the 'progressive' guise of close community involvement the police actively promote surveillance and informing within communities and then record and disseminate all that is gathered.

The appointment of Sir Kenneth Newman as Metropolitan Commissioner was greeted in the media as an indication that Scarman was being taken seriously. He was variously hailed as an 'intellectual', a 'thinker' and a 'strategist'. With a recent background in the hard-line RUC in the north of Ireland as Chief Constable, followed by work on the development of 'new' community-based teaching initiatives as Commandant of Bramshill, Newman was chosen as the person most suitable to strike the balance between reactive, preventive and community-based strategies. Within a short time he confirmed what many critics of the police had been saying for years: that if statistics had indicated anything of substance it was that the police were inefficient in detecting crime. In 1982, for example, the detection rate for recorded crime was a mere 16 per cent. Yet while the critics had called for an explanation for such inefficiency, Newman simply announced that the police could not be expected to do the job. What he proposed was that new community-based initiatives would extend the surveillance function of community policing to include neighbourhood watch schemes.

The public were given an opportunity to sample neighbourhood watch schemes in a TV documentary which followed two British police officers on a fact-finding visit to the USA. In the example shown in the film the local community virtually policed itself. This ranged from information gathering and the reporting of sightings of strangers to the cruising of streets, complete with flashing lights and radio intercom. This again raises the issues of surveillance, information gathering and the dissemination of personal information. Who constitutes a 'suspect', what constitutes a 'suspicious circumstance' and how such information is used are all problems of categorization and classification as individuals are encouraged to act on their prejudices or received stereotypes. With the justification of 'helping communities to help themselves' a scheme is legitimated which actually turns communities in on themselves. Such schemes are not far distant from those which advocate 'community justice' and use vigilantes to enforce and apply the law. Neighbourhood watch, then, constituted a new direction in the use of community policing, and started with four 'pilot' programmes. The initial programme was written up as follows:

> These will start with signs being posted with slogans like, 'This street is patrolled by civilian observation patrols – Met. Police'; the police will be responsible for mobilizing local people and a volunteer co-ordinator will be appointed; residents will be given lists of neighbours' names and telephone numbers, so that checks can be made if anything happens to their property; and household and personal property will be marked to show up under infrared light, based on London postal codes which can identify down to blocks of only six houses. Together this part of the Newman plan will enable the police to have their initiatives legitimated through consultative committees; to incorporate local government and social agencies into their operations; and to gather local 'intelligence' and otherwise to be assisted by the creation of 'vigilante' squads street by street.[22]

The neighbourhood watch scheme was introduced in London in September 1983; by May 1984 with 389 schemes were operational, another 509 schemes in the process of being planned. Early in 1984 Douglas Hurd, a minister of state at the Home Office, stated that the police had selected high crime areas for the schemes, regarding 40 per cent participation of households as the minimum rate for a successful neighbourhood scheme.[23] One early case study, reported in *Policing London*, showed that schemes could be set up against the wishes of people in the community and in a form which did not meet the stated policing needs of the community. The pressure on local communities to take part in the schemes included a crime prevention officer making the following statement to a tenants' association meeting:

> If you do not accept this scheme, we shall simply go down

the road and offer it to the next estate, who will accept it
and the result of that will be that their crime and criminals
will be pushed onto your estate.[24]

By mid-1984, 22 police forces had developed neighbourhood watch
schemes and a further 11 had schemes planned. [25] This widespread
development of neighbourhood watch was supported by a Home
Office publication for police officers on the implementation of the
schemes. A joint departmental circular on crime prevention
emphasized the importance of inter-agency co-operation under
which 'schools, local government and other agencies, as well as the
public, are expected to assist the police, with no additional
resources for the community, to build a safer environment'.[26]

The broad development of the schemes brought reservations
about the availability and use of confidential information on people
and the selection and targeting of particular neighbourhoods. The
much-publicized release in 1982 of crime statistics according to
racial origin did much to consolidate the mythology of black crime
as the *most* quantifiably significant contribution to a 'crime wave'.
It is clear that the community targeting of 'suspicious persons'
follows in the footsteps of racist SPG operations such as 'Swamp
81', and popular white racism is further consolidated and
legitimated by neighbourhood watch schemes.

Thus community policing has come a long way from the Devon
and Cornwall programme under Alderson. All the doubts concerning surveillance, information gathering, record keeping, dissemination and accountability, which initially drew words of
reassurance, have been realized in the new inner-city programmes.
Sold to communities on the basis of greater consultation and a
realistic attempt to combat street crime, the use of community
policing not only sits alongside fire-brigade policing – it provides a
new base for it. In 1982 a senior police officer, David Webb, who
had done much to promote the Alderson strategy in Handsworth,
Birmingham, resigned from the West Midlands Police because he
considered that there was a failure in the force to take the project
seriously. Against this the Chief Constable, Sir Philip Knights,
defended the force and paid tribute to the contribution of
community-policing strategies to better community relations. Again,
it is worth considering the relationship between such reassurances
and some of the recent events in the West Midlands area.

On 1 March 1983 newspapers carried a story which, by any standards, defied credibility. A 64-year-old man had claimed £534 from the West Midlands Police for damages to his property caused by a police 'mistake'. The mistake was that the police had forced entry into the wrong flat. The story of the bungled police raid, however, did little to improve police-community relations in the West Midlands. Using sledgehammers and kicking down doors, the police arrived unannounced in the bedrooms of three old people, including a woman of 90. Not satisfied from appearances that they had made a dreadful mistake, the police forced a 64-year-old man from his bed, spreadeagled him, ordered him from the house and took him to the station. Eventually the man persuaded the police that none of the people who lived at his house was responsible for a series of armed robberies in Wales. The people at the house remained silent about the affair but the Chief Constable offered an ex gratia payment which was £200 less than the cost of the damage. The Vice-Chairman of the Police Committee did not seem too concerned: 'It would be a very odd situation if every police operation like this was entirely successful.'[27] The publicity given to this case soon revealed that it was one of a series of similar errors involving strong-arm tactics against innocent people.

Attention remained focused on the West Midlands Police when a suspect, held in police cells at Coventry, died later in March 1982, after being involved in a struggle with several police officers. Following the police investigation into the death in custody of James Davey, the Director of Public Prosecutions decided not to prosecute any of the officers concerned. Once again the coroner's inquest became the only forum in which the family gained access to any information surrounding James Davey's death. The inquest verdict was death by misadventure but the debate focused attention on the use of force by the police. In October 1983 a Birmingham policeman was imprisoned for kicking, punching and head-butting a handcuffed prisoner. This was followed, in November 1983, by the conviction of three West Midlands detectives who had beaten up a suspect in their custody. A financier, in the same area, spent two days in police cells after wrongly parking his car while he bought a loaf of bread. He was given an absolute discharge by the court.

Perhaps the most controversial case in the West Midlands in 1983 came after a woman, Madeline Haigh, wrote a letter to a newspaper concerning the siting of cruise missiles at Greenham. She received a visit from the Special Branch. After complaining about the visit Ms Haigh was told that no such visit had been made. She pursued the case and eventually the visit was admitted and defended by the Chief Constable. In a statement in early November Sir Philip Knights challenged the popular assumption that the Special Branch concern themselves only with suspected subversive activities. He stated that Branch activities are wide-ranging and include 'many criminal cases *likely* to be committed in the field of public order which have no subversive connotations whatever' (emphasis added). As he was replying to the Haigh case, it can only be assumed that the Chief Constable considered that her letter was sufficient to indicate the *likelihood* of criminal activity. Yet Madeline Haigh's letter bore no reference to any criminal activity, nor could it be constructed as such. The Knights statement was in marked contrast to his comments on Special Branch operations made in his Annual Report a year earlier:

> The Special Branch is not interested *in any way* in legitimate political or industrial activities. The only organizations of interest are those which fall within the *generally* accepted definition of subversion, i.e. activities which threaten the safety or wellbeing of the state and which are intended to undermine or overthrow parliamentary democracy by political, industrial or violent means. (Emphasis added).

Madeline Haigh's letter must therefore have been interpreted as non-legitimate and its contents must have fallen within the 'generally accepted' definition of subversion. Knights' contradictions are in themselves instructive. They exemplify the broad discretion entrusted to the police in their operational duties. Throughout the events the Labour-controlled Police Committee affirmed their support for 'Sir Philip' and appeared reluctant to consider that the unfortunate series of events added up to a crisis in their force.

Even if it is assumed that these cases represent a coincidence of circumstances, there is no doubt that they influence public perceptions of the force. With David Webb's resignation over the status of community policing a well-known controversy, reassurances from the Chief Constable concerning good police-community relations rang hollow. While the public relations police image projected throughout the West Midlands' cities and towns has been one of harmony and community liaison, the reality of reactive policing has told another story.

The apparent contradiction between community policing and reactive policing is well illustrated by the West Midlands' Police Orders, No. 34/1982, 'Monitoring the Potential for Serious Public Disorder', published on 4 May 1982. In these Orders, Sir Philip Knights comments, 'The disorders which took place in the Force area during 1981 highlighted the need for a *monitoring system* which would help to *detect early indications* of community tension which *might foreshadow* serious public disorder' (emphasis added). Police-community relations are then couched in terms of a system 'which relies on the gathering of information from many sources and the subsequent assessment of this information'. The paragraphs which illustrate Knights' interpretation of good community policing are worth considering in full:

1.3 The following warning indicators are suggested as guidelines but are not to be regarded as exhaustive; of equal importance will be the *discerned feelings* of sections of the community which are made known to PBOs (Permanent Beat Officers), Unit Patrol Officers, detectives and members of the Public Liaison Department through a variety of contacts.

1.4 These warning indicators include:

i. increased hostility to police operations, such as the making of arrests;

ii. unusually large groups of youths congregating in public thoroughfares and showing hostility towards the police;

iii. harassment of individual police officers by groups of youths;

iv. increases in the number of assaults on police officers;

v. increases in the number of attacks on police vehicles;

vi. the development of heavy anti-police propaganda and the circulation of rumours and false information about police activities and practices;

vii. increased numbers of complaints against the police, especially of alleged brutality and harassment;

viii. the breaking down of previously established liaison and

138 / The state of the police

consultative arrangements;
ix. increased numbers of complaints of racial attacks and a lack of police response;
x. conflict between or within racial groups particularly conflict involving violence;
xi. incidents which achieve notoriety, such as the arrest of prominent individuals, providing a focus for community discontent.

The Orders state that all information concerned with potential tension in the community should be forwarded to the collator. Clearly, surveillance and information gathering forms a major part of community intervention in Knights' force. The West Midlands Standing Order A5, published in November 1980 and entitled 'Police Community Relations', states that PBOs should become involved with 'problem children', 'marital problems', housing, financial and associated problems. It continues, 'When making contact with such agencies, officers will bring to the notice of the superintendent of the sub-division any criticism of, or hostility towards police which they might encounter during these contacts . . .' In their contacts with schools, divisional public liaison officers are instructed to gather information on 'any abnormal attitudes displayed by the pupils which must require special consideration'. They are also instructed to maintain regular contact with all other agencies, including youth work and the church. The aims of these activities are summarized as follows:

. . . to ensure that *any social situation* developing in the Force area which *could* lead to *any* increase in crime or disorder should not go unnoticed . . . effect can only be given to the policy if officers pay keen attention to the social scene around them and report upon developments *likely to interfere* with the wellbeing of the community in which they are working. (Emphasis added).

The directions are suitably ambiguous and could be extended to include almost any social situation, political meeting, picket, gathering or meeting. The links between the West Midlands' terms of reference and the community-policing strategies discussed earlier are easy to appreciate. The 'targets' of police public liaison emerge in the document without any previous comment: 'if immigrants are to be successfully absorbed into our society, it is extremely important that there should be a firm link between police and other welfare organizations'. Much is made of the anticipation of 'potential areas of conflict', 'community trends' and the assessment of 'existing areas of conflict'.

What the West Midlands' material suggests is that there is no contradiction between the apparently progressive policies of community policing and the much criticized reactive form of police operations. As Newman has argued, they fit together to provide a form of 'total policing'. Both Alderson and Scarman laid the ground for such a combination by endorsing saturation tactics, differential policing and forceful methods. Yet community policing has been adopted, almost without question, by previously critical police committees, the Labour Party, the SDP/Liberal Alliance and a range of other civil libertarian organizations.

Taken in total, the case studies referred to in this chapter indicate that community-policing initiatives are in practice a far cry from progressive police-community relations. The use of such a strategy to 'gain the confidence' of other agencies, key workers in the community and the people themselves, provides the opportunity for a level of targeting and surveillance which no previous strategy could offer. Coupled with the proven lack of political account-ability, it has not only consolidated police autonomy but has also laid the foundation for a form of total policing without effective consultation and with no check on the use of police discretion.

7. A national police force?

'It is no use setting about a police officer, because behind
him stands the police force, behind them the Army, Navy
and Air Force and behind them the whole state.' Mr Justice
McKinnon[1]

1984 added a further dimension to the operational independence of
the police. During the coal dispute the police dispensed with their
own much-acclaimed links with local government. The deployment
of police officers across force boundaries under the national
agreement of 'mutual aid', an initiative developed in response to the
1980-1 uprisings, has become institutionalized under central
direction. This regular deployment was made without any consultation between chief constables and police authorities. It paid no
attention to the statutory duty of police authorities to provide an
adequate and efficient police force for their own communities. It
provided a clear demonstration that the political autonomy of the
police, so obvious in the Merseyside confrontation, has been
consolidated and now has the added dimension of operating within
a nationally co-ordinated framework. In this chapter this shift is
examined within the context of policing industrial conflict since the
confrontation with the miners in 1972. The chapter concludes with
a detailed evaluation of the events of 1984 and the serious issues that
the policing of the pit communities raise for political accountability
of the police in other areas.

The significance of Saltley Gates

In 1968 the Royal Commission on Trade Unions and Employers'
Associations (the Donovan Report) concluded that the use of the
unofficial strike by workers, coupled with the power of shop
stewards, represented a twin threat to industrial order and worker

discipline. The panic which followed the seamen's strike in 1966 had produced a climate in which 'conspirators', union 'agitators' and communist 'militants' were considered to be alive and well and running the unions on the shop floor. In 1969 the Ford management used the courts to defeat their workers and this produced new calls for stronger legislation and new powers which would bring an end to the 'crisis' in industrial relations.

In June 1970 the Heath government came to power on a strong law and order platform which included a 'firm grip' on the unions. Within the year the Tories tabled an Industrial Relations Bill. It was argued that the Bill was a necessity to provide responsible management and responsible unions with a framework in which to conduct responsible negotiations. It was an attack on 'union militants' who were portrayed as destroying the fabric of good industrial relations and causing inflation. Stuart Hall and others considered this 'conspiratorial version' as the 'received political doctrine' in which

> labour was to be disciplined by the *law* – a tight framework of legal constraints in the industrial relations field, backed by courts and fines; an attack on picketing; if necessary, a few exemplary arrests.[2]

The 1971 Act stipulated the formal registration of unions, challenged the closed shop, set up the Industrial Relations Court and restricted the long-held right of workers to withdraw their labour. Union opposition to the Tory legislation grew and more working days were lost through strikes in 1972 than at any time since 1919 and workers used the sit-in as a means of negotiation. Attempts were made to close Upper Clyde Shipbuilders and the Industrial Relations Court ordered access to be given to a transport firm delivering to Liverpool docks. Workers' rights to picket were seriously undermined during the dockworkers' strike and heavy fines were made against the union for contempt. Five London dockers were imprisoned for contempt, the effect of which was to harden worker attitudes and bring widespread support for the union.

The Tory government's determination to outlaw picketing set the trade union movement on a collision course with the government, the courts and, inevitably, the police. The first national miners' strike since 1926 was called in January 1972. Within a month a highly organized mass picket confronted the police at the Saltley Coke Depot in the West Midlands. It was the National Union of Mineworkers' intention to mobilize action which would block the movement of supplies in and out of retail depots. The 'flying pickets' had arrived, committed to secondary action directed against suppliers. It was the government's position that action not directed against an employer but against another business not involved in the dispute should be outside the law.

The week-long confrontation at Saltley, involving nearly 1,000 police and up to 15,000 pickets, at times produced a fierce battle. Arthur Scargill, the Yorkshire miners' leader, wrote that the police used excessive violence against the pickets.[3] He claimed that police were disguised as pickets, that those in uniform covered or removed their numbers and that plain-clothes officers used telescopic cameras to maintain surveillance. The intimidation of pickets hardened the resolve of the miners and the mass picket grew until finally Saltley Gates were closed.

The successful picket at Saltley was hailed as a significant victory for the mass picketing tactics and a serious setback both to the Heath government and to the forceful tactics employed by the police. Politicians and senior military officers called for a voluntary private force to support the police in such confrontations. The use of flying pickets brought renewed demands for stronger laws. A political solution to the dispute was found as Heath argued that the miners constituted a 'special case'.

In 1973 six building workers from Shrewsbury were charged under an 1875 Act with 'conspiracy to intimidate people to abstain from their lawful work'. Their sentences, as high as three years, were severe. On appeal, the court maintained that the sentences represented a deterrent. Conspiracy, it was decided, was a 'matter of inference', 'seldom expressed in words' and those involved need not even know each other. Neither need they have been involved throughout, nor have been aware of the full extent of the conspiracy. A move towards embodying in a new law the kind of practices for which the Shrewsbury pickets were convicted became clear in a speech from the Conservative Secretary of State for Employment, Robert Carr:

I hope that we might get a code of picketing practice, interpreting the law into practical guidance for members of

unions and helping to exclude those people who take part in
these troubles who have nothing to do with them, have
nothing to do with the unions concerned, have no concern
for the good of the work-people and are only there to make
trouble.[4]

The Heath government's use of the law to control the unions and
their members had led to the imprisonment of trade unionists. The
unions were depicted as moving into an extreme form of leftwing
militancy. For their part the unions responded by refusing to
negotiate a political compromise with the Tories, and in February
1974 Heath called a general election to gain the country's support
for his policies. He was defeated.

The Conservatives' defeat in 1974 was inevitably linked to the
closure of Saltley Gates. That one incident was taken as the moment
when the predicted breakdown in law and order, the full-blown
crisis in industrial relations, had arrived. It symbolized the
potential power and solidarity of the unions and demonstrated that
collective action on a large scale could close workplaces. It was also
clear from the Saltley Gates confrontation that the police, regardless
of their use of offensive tactics, were not capable of handling
well-organized mass pickets. While there were demands for legal
controls on mass picketing and for the prevention of flying pickets,
the priority for the police was to establish contingency plans and
appropriate training for the containment and control of picket lines.

The panic that 1972 stimulated at a senior level is well illustrated
in a comment made by Brendan Sewill, special adviser to the
Chancellor of the Exchequer:

Many of those in positions of influence looked into the abyss
and saw only a few days away the possibility of the country
being plunged into a state of chaos not so very far removed
from that which might prevail after a minor nuclear attack.
. . . This is the power that existed to hold the country to
ransom: it was fear of that abyss which had an important
effect on subsequent policy.[5]

The subsequent policy took three directions. First, at centralized
government level, the Civil Contingencies Unit was set up. It was
based at the Cabinet Office and entrusted with long-term

monitoring and immediate response to union disputes in key industries. Second, there was the stated intention of the Heath government to develop a code of practice for picketing, to draft new legislation against the internal workings of the unions and against secondary picketing. Finally, there was the emergence of a policy of mutual aid between police forces with provision for specialist training. This was brought together under the centralized co-ordination and control of the National Reporting Centre (NRC). The person responsible for making the NRC operational at any given time would be the President of the Association of Chief Police Officers (ACPO). Clearly it was intended from the outset that the Civil Contingencies Unit, the Home Secretary, the NRC and the ACPO would work closely together should there be a recurrence of the 1972-4 confrontation. The contingency planning which went into the co-ordination of this initiative was carried out without any public debate and without the knowledge of local police authorities.

Throughout the 1974-9 Labour government the initiative lay dormant, even though there was a major confrontation between the police and mass pickets at Grunwick in 1976. At Grunwick the police again demonstrated their resolve to use forceful means to assist in the breaking of a strike. Unlike Saltley Gates, however, the picket was forcefully contained and the processing factory was kept open. The use of the Special Patrol Group and the violent charges on the pickets brought widespread criticism of police tactics and condemnation by government ministers. The Metropolitan Police showed clearly their sympathies with the Grunwick management. This ranged from the friendly relationships within the factory between the management and the police[6] to comments made by Robert Mark, the Metropolitan Police Commissioner who praised the Grunwick owner: 'An Anglo-Indian running a small business has courageously and successfully stood firm against politically motivated violence on the streets.'[7]

Robert Mark's position on trade union disputes is apparent from his comments on the Shrewsbury pickets. In his opinion they had 'committed the worst of all crimes, worse even than murder'. This was the attempt to 'achieve an industrial or political objective by criminal violence'.[8]

To the Tory opposition Grunwick showed that the trade union movement would use mass picketing again in the furtherance of a dispute. On one day alone 8,000 pickets confronted the police, 113 were arrested and 243 were injured. Grunwick was used, particularly by the media, to fuel the continuing debate about picket-line violence and union power. The dispute began over the right of black workers to join a union. It had the unconditional support of the labour movement, politicians, the law and popular opinion. By the end of the dispute however, attention was focused almost exclusively on the legitimacy of picketing. Hard-line policing, particularly the violence of the SPG, was not considered an important issue as public attention was drawn by the media towards the question of how pickets could be most effectively controlled. The police were seen as the victims of the disorder rather than as main contributors to it.

Following Grunwick, Lord Denning, Master of the Rolls, sharpened the debate on picketing when he challenged the basis of the 'right to strike'. He conluded:

> I would declare at once that there is no such right known to the law, not at any rate when it is used to inflict great harm on innocent bystanders or to bring the country to a halt. So far as the law is concerned, those who do such things are exercising not a right but a great power, the power to strike.[9]

Thus the ground was well laid for the inevitable attack on the unions, their members' right to strike and the freedom to picket. The opportunity for the Tories to 'pick up where they had left off' in 1974 came in 1979 when, after a winter of industrial discontent, the Thatcher government was returned. The 'crisis' had been created and the debate, inevitably, came back to the issue of picketing. The focus was on secondary picketing in particular, with one leading industrialist complaining that he had been subjected to 'psychological picketing'. Within days of its election the Thatcher government outlined its intention to present new and immediate legislation on employment and the unions. The effective control of industrial disputes and the conduct of pickets formed the basis of a Code of Practice, drawn up by the government, and of the 1980 Employment Act. Thus the Tories' determination in 1972 to structure a code of practice on picketing coupled with legal sanctions had been realized. The legacy of Saltley Gates had not been forgotten.

'Beating the pickets'

The 1980 Employment Act and the Code of Practice embodied principles which had long been popular with the police. Robert Reiner quoted findings of a survey into rank-and-file police attitudes which was carried out in the wake of the Saltley Gates confrontation:

> Only 45 per cent of the police felt that the law was adequately enforced at pickets; 36 per cent thought that the existing legal powers of the police were sufficient, but that their senior officers tended to be overinhibited in their enforcement policy because of fear of political repercussions.[10]

Of the officers surveyed a significant number demanded stricter legal control of pickets supported by a more rigorous programme of enforcement. Fifty-one per cent called for tighter overall control of pickets and a substantial minority wanted to see picketing outlawed completely.

Demands for the tight regulation of picketing also came from senior officers. In evidence to the Home Affairs Committee, ACPO requested a clause in the 1980 Employment Act which would set limits on the number of pickets allowed at any given place. The chief officers' association wanted the Act to state that the number of pickets should 'not often' exceed six, and Sir Philip Knights, then Chief Constable of the West Midlands, considered that he could envisage a situation in which two pickets would be too many. The increasing demands for the tight regulation of picket lines was a move well beyond the initial demands for the control of secondary picketing. It was clearly an attack on the established right to picket. An article by Kenneth Sloan, published in *Police Review* at the height of the panic over the 'winter of discontent', reflected the dominant police attitude towards the strikers:

> Members of picket lines are dedicated people who hold strong beliefs in the right of their cause, plus, all too frequently, a few fully paid up members of the 'kick-a-copper' brigade. It is *impossible to reason with either*. As individuals the pickets may be perfectly reasonable, but in

groups they are blinkered and brainwashed by their union representatives and unwilling to show themselves to have *any human feelings* in front of their colleagues.[11] (Emphasis added)

Quite clearly the programme of control envisaged by the 1980 Employment Act and its associated Code of Practice was popular throughout the police force. Under the Act *lawful* picketing was confined to workers in dispute with their employer and who picketed only their place of work. Any other person who attended a picket in sympathy was defined as a 'demonstrator in support of a picket'. The Act provided employers with a *civil* remedy for secondary picketing; the *criminal* law remained unchanged. Effectively, as Patricia Hewitt wrote, the Act plus the police discretion embodied in the Code of Practice provided the framework by which 'trades unionists taking part in entirely peaceful protest'[12] could be made criminals. The Code of Practice stated that there were no specific limits on the number of pickets at any one place and it re-inforced the principle that the number permissible should remain at the discretion of the police on duty at the time. Picket organizers were advised, however, that as a general rule the number of pickets should not exceed six at any entrance. Effectively the control and regulation of a picket was left to the police. They should use their discretionary powers to respond to any situation as they saw fit. Inevitably this meant the use of powers of arrest for 'obstruction', 'obscene language', 'assault', 'actions likely to cause a breach of the peace' and other suitably ambiguous uses of the common law.

The notion that the police in industrial disputes were impartial enforcers of just law was further exposed in 1981 at a picket line at the Laurence Scott Engineering Works in Greater Manchester. Throughout a long dispute pickets had succeeded in halting all access to the works. It had been a bitter dispute but there had been no major confrontation and no violence. However, early one morning large numbers of Greater Manchester police suddenly appeared on the streets around the works. Requests for information by the 20-plus pickets were met with grim silence. Later in the day two helicopters landed in the Scott works and airlifted goods and equipment out of the works. The operation enabled essential parts to be delivered to Scott's frustrated customers and the strike was effectively broken.

The pickets and their unions were outraged that the Greater Manchester Police, at a senior operational level, were part of the planning and protection of a clearly provocative act of strike-breaking. Following a complaint to the Greater Manchester Police Committee, the point was taken up by Committee members who severely criticized the Chief Constable, James Anderton. For if the operation warranted the deployment of police in such large numbers then it was clear that the airlift was intimidatory and likely to cause a breach of the peace. Once again it was apparent that the common law powers vested in the police would be reserved solely for use against pickets. Anderton's officers had used their discretion to protect the interests of an employer and had placed greater emphasis on these interests than on the interests of a lawful picket. Anderton's response was characteristic. He criticized, once again, the Police Committee for attempting to undermine the authority and professional judgement of the police. As he stated, the 'warning bells are now ringing' as the door had been opened 'to those whose sole aim is political direction and control of the police and the removal of independence and power from the chief constables'.[13]

In November 1983 the police response to a mass picket in Warrington produced clear evidence that a wind of change had blown through contemporary policing. The mass picket was an attempt to prevent the movement of the *Warrington Messenger* free newspaper. Its proprietor, Eddie Shah, had sacked six workers in a dispute involving the replacement of unionized labour by non-unionized labour. His version of the events, supported by the rightwing press and by Tory politicians, was that it was a dispute over workers' rights *not* to join a union – the National Graphical Association. The opposing view, which was held throughout the trade union movement, was that Shah was attempting to break the union and to undercut union agreed wage rates and conditions of employment.

The union called for a mass picket each week on the one night that Shah delivered his newspapers from the factory. The only concern of the police was to ensure that the delivery vans would be able to leave the factory unimpeded. As with the Grunwick dispute, where the police restrained a mass picket in order to allow non-strikers to enter the factory in buses, the Warrington confrontation was portrayed as the police enabling an employer to go about his lawful business. From the outset of the dispute it was clear that the police intended to side with the employer in their selective enforcement of law on the picket line.

What was unusual about the Warrington dispute was that the Home Secretary, Leon Brittan, reacted early in the dispute. He advised the Chief Constable of the Cheshire Police that he could call in specialist reinforcements from other forces as and when he considered necessary. Nevertheless, it would still be the primary responsibility of the Cheshire Police Committee to bear the costs of policing the dispute, including overtime and reinforcements from other forces. Yet Brittan acted without formal consultation with the Police Committee on whose statutory authority any decision concerning the financing of operational decisions should have been made. While a 60 per cent police grant was guaranteed from the Home Office for the costs of policing the dispute, Brittan's assurance to the Cheshire Chief Constable denied the authority of the Police Committee. A second important factor in Brittan's response was that it became clear that contingency plans now existed for the deployment between forces of specially trained riot-control officers. The 1980-1 uprisings had brought not only changes in training and equipment for riot control, but also changes in the planning for such situations. These contingency plans – the deployment of specialist resources to situations of 'high tension', as defined by the 'tension indicators' discussed in the last chapter – announced the arrival of a national police response to 'civil disorder'. The move towards a centrally co-ordinated police response to large-scale industrial conflict, first programmed after Saltley Gates, was now a working reality. Mutual aid, under central co-ordination and with Home Office support, undermined the political responsibilities of local policing.

The strategies adopted by the police at Warrington for handling the picket also showed that lessons had been learned from the street battles of 1980-1. An important element in this was the early use of riot police and their aggressive style of controlling the picket. The events of the night of 29 November showed what the police response was to be. As the pickets arrived and attempted to push back the massed ranks of police officers, anyone in the front two lines of pickets was liable to be 'snatched' at random. Eyewitnesses on the front lines claimed that the police 'pummelled' those they pulled out and arrested some without any specific reason. A regional secretary of a teachers' union gave the following account of the next sequence of events which centred on the NGA caravan which the union were using to marshall the picket:

> Police had entered it. I could hear crashing noises and shouts. Someone shouted, 'Stop 'em, they're breaking up the equipment.' A TV cameraman put floodlights on the door. A police voice warned him to put out the light. There was a crashing sound and I could see equipment being thrown out of the caravan.[14]

The NGA van, which by using radio was the only means whereby the union officials could effectively control the picket, was then overturned. This incensed the pickets but already the police were into the next phase. Behind the lines of police officers the riot police were formed up.

> Suddenly all hell let loose. I thought I was in a different land. The faceless robots [a reference to the riot equipment] simply charged through an opening in the police ranks and waded through a dense pack of pickets 'like a dose of salts'. Having got through, they charged up the road, scattering the observers, regardless of where they were, participating or not. They chased us across fields. Later they chased some with land rovers right up to the motorway . . . I had been shocked at having to run for my life. There was no doubt they truncheoned anyone who came in their path, running or standing – everyone was a target simply by being there.

From this point on the situation deteriorated. A police car, driven at speed across the site, crashed and was stoned. A telegraph pole was uprooted and the lines came down on the police. There was no direction by the marshalls because the communications van had been 'dismantled' by the police. The riot squads, in groups of 20 and more, snatched people indiscriminately. Many pickets were beaten. For many people who went to Warrington this was their first experience of a mass picket. It was the common view that 'police provocation and tactics of violence' had created a major confrontation. Few people had ever experienced the paramilitary strategies adopted by the police that night. The handling of the pickets, the systematic destruction of the NGA communications van and the early introduction of the riot squads added up to a carefully planned police operation. Riot equipment, previously associated with defensive, last-resort strategies, was elevated at Warrington to an offensive, first-choice strategy of control and punishment. This shift, a direct result of the 1980-1 uprisings, signalled the arrival in mainland Britain of a highly organized and blatantly aggressive mode of policing public order.

The Warrington confrontation also illustrated that the new strategies for handling industrial disputes, derived from discreet consultations between the Home Office and chief constables, were part of a national plan. This national initiative placed political decisions concerning the handling of sensitive disputes above the authority and influence of local government. Although local police authorities have statutory control over the financing of police work in their areas, they have no say in operational decisions and priorities. The chief constables have agreed on national priorities in consultation with a Tory government. The local police authorities are responsible for meeting the cost of operations but they result from consultations in which they have no say.

The costs of policing the Warrington picket were substantial. Figures presented to the Cheshire Police Committee showed an overall cost of £314,000. Yet this did not cause the Tory leader of Cheshire County Council to question the police operation. Rather it was his feeling that the NGA should have been sued for the cost of policing the picket. For the local police authority to find such a substantial sum, which had not been budgeted for, other previously agreed projects and priorities had to be foregone. This applied also to other forces which had sent reinforcements. The use of police from other forces, without consultation with their police authorities, inevitably had an effect on the efficiency of police operations in the home force areas. Attempts in West Lancashire, however, to gain information about the deployment of Lancashire Police at Warrington and the effect on efficiency levels in the county drew a 'no comment' from the Chief Constable at the newly constituted police-community liaison committee. He justified this by arguing that it was an operational matter and such information would not be given to the Police Committee or County Council. Effectively the Tory government's initiative for policing industrial disputes again denied political accountability to local government.

The NGA was crippled financially by the court awards made

against the union for the mass picket at Warrington. If the purpose of successive Tory Employment Acts had been to break trade unionism, then the NGA dispute showed the effectiveness of the new law in doing just that. After the dispute the NGA was left almost bankrupt, unable to fulfil its normal welfare and pension obligations to its members and their families.

Policing the miners

When picketing began over the pit closure programme, the National Coal Board (NCB) appeared reluctant to use the courts to prevent action by the miners. This decision, particularly in relation to pits where miners were working, was part of a political strategy. In a television interview, Lord Denning argued that it was a matter of 'high policy', a decision taken by senior cabinet ministers, that the courts had not been used. Instead the strategy chosen was to 'call out hundreds and thousands of police'.[15] Peter Hennessy of the Policy Studies Institute, whose work has involved monitoring the government's response to industrial disputes in key industries, agreed that there was a well-established government strategy of confrontation with the miners. The first phase of this strategy was to build up coal stocks, particularly at power stations, as a deterrent to a strike. The second phase was, in the event of a strike, to encourage the NCB to 'buy time' in the hope that there would be a drift back to work. Finally, private hauliers would be used to do any necessary moving of stocks or material, thus keeping the troops out of the dispute. For this strategy to be successful, according to Hennessy, the 'police will have to take the brunt in the front line'.[16]

Thus the pressure was immediately on the police. It was their responsibility to regulate and control the pickets throughout the coalfields. This included securing the unhindered passage of supplies nationally and keeping all relevant depots open. As John Alderson stated, the Thatcher government was determined that Saltley Gates should not be repeated and it was up to the police to make sure that this did not happen. The primary objective of the police was to reduce the effectiveness of the mass picket. For several weeks Nottinghamshire was virtually sealed off as the police prevented the free movement of vehicles in and through the county. Any vehicles driven by men suspected of being 'flying pickets' were stopped at motorway turn-offs and on other main routes into Nottinghamshire and turned back. Failure to comply with police instructions brought instant arrest. The long-distance record for 'action likely to cause a breach of the peace' was claimed by the Kent Police when they turned back miners and their supporters, travelling north, at the Dartford Tunnel.

In a *TV Eye* documentary on the policing of the dispute Charles McLachlan, the Chief Constable of Nottinghamshire, stated that the use of roadblocks had been his personal initiative in order to prevent mass picketing in the county. He argued that roadblocks were part of a purposeful strategy aimed at protecting the right of miners to go to work. When confronted with the claim that he was effectively denying the civil rights of individuals to move freely he responded angrily: 'Supporting the freedom of people who want to prevent people going to work is not supporting freedom, but supporting anarchy, violence, riot and damage and everything else.'[17] McLachlan's position was clearly established. For him the 'right to work' far outweighed the 'right to picket', to the extent that striking miners involved in attempts to persuade peacefully those determined to break the strike were identified automatically with 'anarchy, violence, riot and damage'. It was on this basis that the Chief Constable, destined to become the President of ACPO, turned the County of Nottinghamshire into an island governed in effect by unofficial pass laws. After MPs raised questions concerning the use of the police national computer in the operation, it was disclosed that vehicles belonging to pickets had been logged in the stolen and suspect vehicles index of the PNC.

The use of roadblocks had been discussed and ratified at a high-level meeting on 9 February 1984 at the Home Office. Following the NGA mass picket, discussions were held between the Home Secretary, the Attorney General and the members of ACPO. These centred on the legal status of roadblocks as a means of halting flying pickets. It was the Attorney General's opinion that the use of roadblocks would be upheld in the courts. Effectively the police were given the go-ahead to use roadblocks to prevent the movement of any people suspected of travelling to a picket line.

The implications of this meeting went far beyond the specific use of roadblocks. John Alderson, the former Chief Constable of Devon and Cornwall, further disclosed that meetings between the Home Secretary, Home Office advisers and members of ACPO had been a regular occurrence throughout both Thatcher administrations.

Such consultations, concerned with major policy initiatives, had taken place not only without the knowledge of Parliament, but also without the knowledge of police authorities throughout the country. The connection between the Civil Contingencies Unit, based at the Cabinet, and the national initiatives internal to ACPO had been well established and operationalized on a regular basis.

Early in the dispute the police disclosed that 'central co-ordination' of operations was taking place at the National Reporting Centre (NRC) based at Scotland Yard. The NRC, set up in 1973 after Saltley Gates, was activated on 13 March 1984 under the direction of ACPO President, David Hall. Within an hour of picketing starting in Nottinghamshire, over 1,000 police officers were, according to David Hall, drafted from outside forces. The main objective of the NRC was to provide instant mutual aid to areas of 'high tension' from forces throughout the country. Of particular concern was the rapid mobilization of specially riot-trained police support units. Thus the role of the NRC has been to maintain close surveillance on pickets, union organizers and strike supporters and to record all movements of pickets. With information carefully gathered and put through the computer to the NRC, the areas of 'high tension' were located and the PSUs deployed. In the first four months of its operation the NRC was responsible for the deployment of approximately 5,500 officers per day. The maximum of 8,100 was reached on 18-19 June. The NRC's 24-hour operation was described as follows:

> Its communications team of seven seconded Metropolitan
> Police officers feeds information into a computer which
> keeps a full record of available resources and demands for
> manpower, right along one wall are charts and lists of PSU
> deployments, a separate chart logs the number of pickets in
> the sites involved. The 'mood' in each area is classified as
> 'peaceful', 'hostile' or 'violent'.[18]

According to *Policing London*, the first ten weeks of the dispute brought '22,000 assignments from a pool of 13,500 men'.[19]

In June the then President of ACPO, David Hall, stated that 'there are no operational directions given from this centre'.[20] The police continued to promote the NRC as nothing more than a clearing house for mutual aid. On BBC's *Newsnight*, Charles

McLachlan, who was not only Nottingham's Chief Constable, but also the new President of ACPO and the co-ordinator of the NRC, denied claims that the NRC was a national police control centre:

> Now look, we've answered this so many times and really you get sick of it, because it is not centrally co-ordinated – the activity – what is centrally co-ordinated is the provision of mutual aid in large numbers between forces who are helping those who need the assistance, and that is what is centrally co-ordinated. The control of police forces is very much under the chief constable in whose area they are active.[21]

There is a fine line between the strategy of deployment and mutual aid, which is nationally co-ordinated, and the control and use of the PSUs which are deployed at any given time. As mutual aid is requested and supplied by chief constables and it is their President who centrally co-ordinates their deployment, the issue of control becomes academic. And the discretion to deploy will be used solely in one direction. On *Newsnight* Chief Constable McLachlan stated that the police 'have to stand in this dispute between the oppressor and the oppressed', by which he meant the striking miners and the working miners. Earlier in the dispute he warned the Nottingham-shire Police Committee of where its allegiances lie. He warned:

> Who am I to serve? Am I to serve the people who are coming in to attack Nottinghamshire people and beat the living daylights out of them if they get a chance, or do I serve the people who are being beaten? I serve the people who are being beaten, and this Committee does too, and don't forget it![22]

The climate in which the police response emerged was set by public statements and warnings such as these and they have been part of the shared politics of policing at a senior level. In this climate, as James Anderton and Kenneth Oxford have repeatedly commented, Labour-controlled police committees have not been trusted. The consequences have been dire, as George Moores, Chairperson of the South Yorkshire Police Committee, stated:

> Up to 13 March we had our normal, full consultation with

our Chief Constable but the NRC was brought into being on the 13 March and from that day onwards we have had no consultation, only information passed on to us. I believe that the chief constables have surrendered their operational independence to the NRC; in other words, the creation of a paramilitary police state.[23]

At no time were local police authorities involved in negotiations about the national policing of the coal dispute. Margaret Simey, Chairperson of the Merseyside Police Committee, considered the chief constables to be 'out of democratic control. It is frightening.'[24] Yet, as with the NGA dispute, chief constables have committed local police committees to massive expenditure. Figures produced in May 1984 [25] showed that up to 27 April Derbyshire had spent £3.2 million and that the North Wales Police estimated their costs to be £350,000 per week. Hampshire, one of the police forces which provided support to others, spent £315,700 in two months and estimated a further 'knock-on' effect within the county to be £70,000 per month. It was the Hampshire Police which chartered a Boeing 737 to fly 126 police officers to Nottinghamshire in order to save the extra overtime payments which would have been made had the officers travelled by road. Nottinghamshire, the target of most of the picketing, placed the cost by May 1984 at nearly £14 million. This figure did not include the claims from other forces for the provision of mutual aid. The Chief Constable of Nottinghamshire considered that as a result of bearing the costs of policing the coal dispute the force would inevitably be less efficient. Margaret Simey of Merseyside stated: 'We have got a bill for £1,750,000 in connection with providing mutual aid already, and it is galloping up every day . . . I am alarmed that no one is totting up the cost of this dispute.'[26]

The lack of consultation with police committees extended beyond the financing of the dispute. As Margaret Simey stated elsewhere: 'it wasn't until a few days after the dispute began, and it occurred to me to ring up and ask if our police were involved, that we knew anything about it. We were never informed, and we are still not informed.'[27] The police authorities, she argued, had no say in the deployment of their forces or the expenditure incurred by the authority. The response of the South Yorkshire Police Committee was to place financial restrictions on its Chief Constable. The

Attorney General brought a successful action against the Police Committee and the position which was upheld in the High Court is clear from his Counsel's argument:

> The Attorney General's concern is to ensure that law and order are maintained and that the Chief Constable is enabled to discharge his responsibilities by being given what he requires for his operational responsibilities over which he has sole control.

According to Margaret Simey, when a representative of Merseyside's Chief Constable was asked by the Police Committee for details of deployment to other forces, he said:

> 'Oh, you'll have to ask the chief that.' But the chief isn't there . . . When we passed a formal resolution asking him to cease sending support units to the strike, he laughed out loud at us and said he wasn't going to take any notice. We wanted a daily breakdown of the number of officers getting overtime, the numbers in Nottingham and so on. You would have thought that was simple enough, it must all be in the books. But he won't give it to us. To this day we only have rough figures.[28]

It was the Police Committee's concern that rate-capping, together with cuts in the police budget imposed by the Department of the Environment, would force them into an illegal budget supported by an illegal rate increase. By July 1984 the total budget for the following year already had been fully committed. Set against this 'forced hand' were the apparently closed consultations between ACPO and the Home Secretary. Margaret Simey stated:

> We know ACPO told all chief constables in writing that they had the Home Secretary's assurance that resources for policing the miners' dispute were not a problem. In other words they were given a blank cheque. But he [the Home Secretary] never told us that. He just walks about saying it's nothing to do with him. It seems ACPO can communicate with the Home Secretary about spending money but not with us. ACPO, in fact, has become an executive limb of the

> state, without any authorization and without being under
> any control. It's incredible.[29]

Margaret Simey believed that the 'principle of government between local, central and the professional' had not only been abandoned but 'wrecked'. Local policing, including the day-to-day cover of the community, was rejected for a central government supported strategy worked out by ACPO and orchestrated by the NRC.

The experience of the Greater Manchester Police Committee closely paralleled that of Merseyside. Its Chairperson, Gabrielle Cox, argued that the coal dispute 'highlighted the fact that chief constables can do what they like'.

> . . . it is not just a question of making an operational
> decision but of making decisions which in the long term will
> affect other public service priorities. Whereas chief
> constables would normally expect to make their decisions
> within the context of a budget, now they are making them
> out of the context of any budget whatsoever . . . We are the
> ones who are having to sign a blank cheque.[30]

Again, the concerns of the Police Committee included the long-term effects on the budget, the proper policing of the community while officers were deployed elsewhere, the lack of information from the Chief Constable and his continual reluctance to involve members in consultation. Gabrielle Cox reported that the Chief Constable, James Anderton, refused to respond on the issue of supplying support units to the strike. She said, 'I suspect his view is that it is nothing to do with us . . . This points up the anomaly that chief constables can virtually do as they like. Our responsibilities appear to be meaningless.'

The coal dispute has shown, as did the NGA dispute in 1983, that police authorities have no control over the expenditure of chief constables in their policy decisions. As the actual police decisions concerning the handling of pickets are operational decisions, the financial implications of taking those decisions are taken out of the hands of the police authorities. The police portray this as a healthy state of affairs since, they argue, this puts their decisions above political control. In the light of the Tory initiative for policing industrial disputes, however, the issue of political affiliation has to be raised. What the above account of the police responses to the coal dispute underlines is that a strategy of *national* proportions exists, is well co-ordinated and has been developed in close consultation, if not direction, with the Tory government. Concern over this relationship was expressed even by *Police Review*: 'The police service is entitled to wonder whether it is being used to preserve law and order or to implement government policy.'[31]

In the course of the 'preservation of law and order', police tactics were all-embracing and hard-line. During the early days of the dispute there were extensive allegations of telephone tapping and close surveillance. Women in South Wales reported that every time they attempted to book a minibus to go campaigning or collecting money out of the area the police knew of the trips and followed. Striking miners alleged that police officers were on the picket lines disguised as pickets and that soldiers were involved in the police operation disguised as police officers. Failure to obey the most trivial police direction – turning back at roadblocks, stepping on or off the pavement, moving on, or even the use of the word 'scab' – often brought immediate arrest under a whole range of charges.

By September 1984 over 7,000 pickets had been arrested with over half charged for 'breach of the peace' under Section 5 of the 1936 Public Order Act. A quarter of those arrested were charged with obstructing a police officer, 11 per cent with obstructing the highway, 10 per cent with criminal damage and 6 per cent with assault on the police. While the media amplified every act of picket-line violence and portrayed the striking miners as thugs who would not stop short of brutality or even murder, the Home Office figures did not bear this out. Acts of severe violence, the beatings of two working miners and the death of a taxi driver did take place. The image of rampaging mobs, however, was not given substance in the figures. Eighty-four per cent of the charges related to breach of the peace or obstruction and would normally be considered trivial offences.

A further important conclusion to be drawn from the charges brought by the police is that they almost exclusively related to offences which were at the discretion of the individual officer. In most cases the evidence of an offence being committed was solely police evidence and the judgement involved (i.e. breach of the peace, obstruction, assault on the police) could only have been made at the time. In that sense the command which regularly echoed across the picket lines – 'Take prisoners!' – was a command almost guaranteed success in the courts. Of the 1,386 cases heard by September, often before stipendiary magistrates from outside the area, 81 per cent were convicted.

The most alarming use of the courts during 1984, and one clearly dictated by the climate of violence engendered in the media and reinforced by the statements of senior police officers, centred on the imposition of blanket bail conditions. With so many cases awaiting the courts and the use of 'flying magistrates' to reduce the backlog, cases took months to come before the court. This led to a new strategy of imposing conditions to the granting of bail on even the most trivial of charges. It was clearly a centrally co-ordinated strategy because the bail conditions were applied in all cases and were typed out on mass-produced forms and clipped to charge sheets. The conditions effectively prevented those charged from taking any further part in the dispute, banning them from picket lines and demonstrations. Solicitors representing miners were strong in their condemnation of the practice:

> It is not a crime to picket at all. There is no criminal offence of picketing. What you have had is something like 6,000 miners arrested during the course of this dispute charged, in the main with minor offences . . . and they are then appearing in court and because of very stringent bail conditions that are being imposed, these men are being prevented, because of the fear of arrest, from taking any part whatsoever in picketing activities again.[32]

> It is a serious subversion of that system when cases are prejudged and decisions made in secret in this way. The ensuing court proceedings are nothing more than a show trial.[33]

A representative of the Nottinghamshire Probation Service commented that exceptional court procedures were adopted which dealt with people purely as a 'matter of expediency'. The mass hearings of cases at all hours was, he said, nothing less than 'supermarket justice'. According to Martin Walker, who monitored the use of the criminal justice system throughout the dispute, a militarized form of policing was supported by courts which were responding as though normal procedures had been suspended. Miners charged with the most routine offences reported being held for up to 28 hours, fingerprinted, photographed and interrogated often in a most hostile manner. The same form of questioning, adopted as routine throughout the strike, had little to do with the often trivial nature of the charges. In the main such interrogation focused on the miners' political affiliations, their friendships and their routine habits.

The 'law and order' climate creates a context in which this form of interrogation is easily justified. The generalization of a violent imagery, with the miners identified as undermining democracy and oppressing their fellow workers, creates the spectre of a 'threat to the state'. Within this climate the use of paramilitary policing, the imposition of virtual curfews, the strategy of mass arrests, the setting of blanket bail conditions and the theme of 'subversion' which ran through interrogations were identified as the necessary, albeit exceptional, precautions to a situation likely to bring down the entire political and economic system. The Thatcher administration played this card to full effect in November 1984.

On 26 November the Home Secretary and the Prime Minister made simultaneous speeches on the coal dispute. Leon Brittan had no doubts as to the main aim of the strike. He stated of the NUM leader:

> Mr Scargill does not just hate our free and democratic
> system and seeks to do everything he can to discredit and
> damage it; he also feels equal hatred and contempt for the
> miners whose servant he is meant to be and whose tyrant he
> has become.[34]

Brittan's comments consolidated the well-established anti-Scargill position of the media. He accused the NUM President of refusing to prevent striking miners from using violence against working miners, their families and their protectors – the police. He concluded: 'it shows all the world with crystal clarity where the *moral responsibility* for the violence lies.' Leon Brittan was intent on identifying Arthur Scargill as both a criminal and a tyrant. He was not only depicted as defying the law, being in contempt over sequestration, but was accused also of actively encouraging violence. A parallel was quickly drawn between Scargill and Hitler: both power-crazed dictators who held the minds of their supporters with little more than rhetoric and fear. One report likened the Yorkshire NUM rallies to fascist rallies in thirties' Germany. The point was not lost on Margaret Thatcher whose November speech contained a virulent attack on the 'fascist Left'. Her generalization of picket-line violence was symptomatic of something far more sinister: the subversion of democracy and the destruction of the rule of law. These constituted for her the 'very dangers we face in Britain today'. She continued:

> At one end of the spectrum are the terrorist gangs within our borders and the terrorist states which arm them. At the other are the hard Left, operating inside our system, conspiring to use union power and the apparatus of local government to break, defy and subvert the laws. Now the mantle has fallen on us to conserve the very principle of parliamentary democracy and the rule of law itself.[35]

It was the Prime Minister's clear intention to put the legitimate use of union power and the properly constituted apparatus of local government in the category of the 'hard Left' and to equate this with political terrorism. Democratically elected union officials involved in their lawful right of organising pickets at their place of work democratically elected local councils which saw fit to support the strike were moulded together with acts of terrorism and presented as the 'enemy within'. The Prime Minister's speech showed clearly that she defined the Tory Party's destiny as being the saviour of parliamentary democracy and the rule of law.

The government's direct involvement in working out a strategy for breaking the strike seems beyond question. Furthermore, it depended on the police playing a central role. For if the NCB and the Tory government were to 'buy time', maintain coal stocks and await the gradual return to work then miners had to be encouraged to break the strike. Miners 'on the brink' of a return to work were not only identified and offered strong financial inducements, they were visited by NCB officials and police officers and guaranteed a safe passage regardless of the size of the inevitable picket.

The 1984-5 confrontation between the police and the miners has underlined the class nature of British policing. The law and order ideology, so evident in the Margaret Thatcher/Leon Brittan speeches and so clear in the statements of senior police officers and ACPO, showed a clear coincidence of interests. It permeated the thinking of the police involved on the picket lines and their selective enforcement of the law. It was present in the courts where bail conditions and payment of costs were used as forms of direct punishment. It was reinforced by an almost universally hostile media and a persistently biased news coverage of the dispute. As part of a process of regulation which controls and contains any resistance to the structural, political and economic inequalities inherent in British society, police operations, priorities and cause practices are yet again firmly rooted in the interests of employers and their political representatives.

8. Responding to the state of the police

In August 1984 Margaret Simey argued that the police 'are out of democratic control'. She stated:

> . . . they have this old code of values that says it's right to be honest, it's right to work, it's wrong to be unemployed. Think of walking the streets of Liverpool with that philosophy; all these unemployed are by definition criminal, morally if not legally, and therefore you approach them as criminals. And before they have time to do anything you hit them on the nose. And when they hit back you've got them, you arrest them . . . It is his [the Chief Constable's] personal responsibility that our officers are involved in what is said to be brutal policing. He doesn't share that with anybody. That is not democracy, especially when that one man is a policeman. I am frightened at where we are headed . . . Even in my most optimistic moments I can see no escape from Ulster . . . [1]

The day after these comments were published, 12 August 1984, the television news showed horrific scenes of brutal policing by the Royal Ulster Constabulary. In a supposed attempt to arrest the banned Publicity Director of Noraid at a small demonstration, the RUC were shown to fire rounds of plastic bullets into the crowd, most of whom were on the ground. They used batons without discrimination. One man, John Downes, was killed – hit in the chest at close range by a plastic bullet. The *Daily Mail* published a photograph showing him at the moment he was hit. An RUC officer stood, a few feet away, apparently firing directly at him. The people, including children at the demonstration with parents, were brutally batoned as they dived for cover from plastic bullets. Photographers, reporters and televison crews received the same treatment. According to reports the demonstration had been without incident and there had been no exceptional provocation. Paul Johnson of the *Guardian* reported that as the RUC left the scene laughter could be heard from within their vehicles.[2] With the exception of the Tory government, the incident brought immediate condemnation from all other parties. The Liberal leader, David Steel, not known for his criticism of police excesses, considered the incident to be an 'unjustifiable police riot . . . involving as it did brutality, injury and death to a crowd which included women and children'. Shirley Williams drew parallels with the Peterloo massacre. The public outrage generated by the visual impact of the police operation demanded an explanation.

The Thatcher government carefully sidestepped the issue of the police action with an admission by the Secretary of State for Northern Ireland, James Prior, which acknowledged that there had perhaps been a mistake in the decision to ban Galvin. The lack of comment on the police operation suggested that given that the ban on Galvin was in existence and he made an appearance then the police behaved reasonably in firing on and batoning the crowd. On 14 August the Chief Constable of the RUC, Sir John Hermon, gave a press conference. His response to many of the reporters who had actually witnessed the events typified the arrogant disdain for their critics and confidence in their political autonomy which now characterizes so many of the UK's chief constables. Despite overwhelming evidence to the contrary, which included television coverage of the Downes killing, Hermon stated that his officers were under serious attack and that they fired only into the air. He dismissed public outrage over the killing of John Downes with a plastic bullet by claiming that he had been identified as 'a member of a party who was rioting'.[3] This statement appeared to suggest that John Downes brought death upon himself. It also emphasized the principle that the police had used their professional discretion to decide upon the level of force 'reasonable' in the circumstances. The people of Ireland's six northern counties were not surprised by the events which stunned so many on the mainland; nor are they surprised that a chief constable would seek to defend RUC brutality. They have lived through internment, armed occupation, house raids, the suspension of the rule of law and the indiscriminate use of state violence. The brutalities of the RUC at Castlereagh and the use of torture to secure confessions were also denied by the previous

Chief Constable, Sir Kenneth Newman. Yet despite the exposure of his denials by the judgement of the European Court, Sir Kenneth Newman moved on to become the Commissioner for the Metropolitan Police.

It is from these events and the police response to them, so typical of the British state's aggressive role in Ireland, that Margaret Simey fears that there is no escape. As the preceding chapters have shown, neither is there any escape from the violence and racism so deeply institutionalized in the main urban police forces; nor from CS gas, plastic bullets and a universally armed police force; nor from the highly technological, centralized form of policing which denies governments, local or national, any say in the policing of the people they represent. To that extent the state of the police is that they have achieved the political autonomy at an operational level necessary to put them beyond democratic control and accountability. The law is no longer in their keeping, it is in their possession.

The debate on the political autonomy of the police and the move towards the centralization of operational policies happened very quickly during the period 1979-85. However, events in the coalfields overtook the emerging debate about the position of police operations and practices in relation to local government. Just as the question of democratic policing in the inner cities was being raised, politically autonomous policing in the coalfields changed entirely the terms of the debate.

Much of the initial critical response to the police favoured changes which would extend the powers of police authorities and curb the autonomy of the chief constables.[4] The discussion in Chapter 6 of the ill-fated Straw Bill shows, however, that any mild extension of police authority powers would be met with strong opposition from ACPO and the Police Federation. Despite reassurances to the contrary, the demand for greater political accountability embodied in this Bill was persistently portrayed by the police as a demand for direct political control and interference in day-to-day operational practices.

On Merseyside, following publication of the Scarman Report and the internal report on police-community relations, there were signs that the serious differences between the Police Committee and its Chief Constable had been settled. An agreement that the Chief Constable would consult with the Police Committee concerning future programmes for policing was hailed as a step forward for 'partnership policing'. Late in 1983, however, the Chairperson of the Police Committee, Margaret Simey, wrote that all this agreement meant was that the Chief Constable made the policy decisions while the Committee paid the bills.[5]

Within months credibility in the 'partnership policing' programme was shattered by the Chief Constable's lack of consultation over the deployment of Merseyside police officers to the coalfields.

It was this lack of willingness by chief constables to move towards a framework in which police committees could play an effective part which sapped credibility in the emerging campaign for political accountability of the police. The setting up of community consultation, as recommended by Lord Scarman, was hailed as a positive development towards better police-community relations. Yet, as the West Lancashire example quoted in Chapter 6 shows, the police-public liaison committees were tightly controlled by the police in terms of what was considered suitable for discussion and what information the Chief Constable considered appropriate to give. Consultation remains a far cry from accountability.

There have been calls for an effective framework of community policing [6] within which the police could be made accountable to the community.[7] Arguing against 'Left idealism' – a position somewhat artificially created by the authors – John Lea and Jock Young have presented a forceful position which they label 'Left realism'. Their argument is that working-class communities suffer disproportionately from the effects of all kinds of crime. They also suffer from a lack of appropriate or effective policing. What is needed is effective policing which responds to the real needs of the community. It is to be developed in close consultation with the community and should ultimately be accountable to the community. The irresponsible 'Left idealists' are portrayed as seeing crime as 'radical struggle "criminalized" by the state and the media'. Their main objective is 'to keep the police out of working-class communities and constantly expose and publicize their repressive actions'.[8] The 'Left realist' position recognizes that 'working-class crime is directed against working-class people' and seeks to promote a 'community-wide' debate on crime, public order and traffic problems enabling 'the community to draw up a clear account of its policing needs'. With a 'new source of cohesion in the local community' engendered by the debate, a 'positive plan for the distribution of police resources would be drawn up'. The debate and the plan would be consolidated through the establishment of a democratically accountable police force, 'one that is trusted by the community'. With mutual trust established the community would then 'yield a high flow of information concerning crime' to its new partner-in-consent: the police. Lea and Young provide no real clue as to how this radical change in partnership policing could take place in the present climate, except to comment that 'democratic accountability requires, at the very least, legislation by a future Labour government'.[9]

In 1984, at the height of the debate over the political accountability of the police, Leslie Curtis, the Chairman of the Police Federation, commented that he could envisage a situation in which it would be impossible for the police to work with a future Labour government. Given the massive resistance by both ACPO and the Police Federation to local political accountability, it would seem most unlikely that a 'future Labour government' could achieve the democratic policing framework envisaged by Lea and Young.

There are also serious doubts about the hopeful claims made by Lea and Young for the establishment of social cohesion within and across working-class community boundaries. The very crimes which reflect the real effects of economic and political marginalization – including racial violence and sexual assault – will not be so easily overcome by the 'great community debate'. Yet Lea and Young remain optimistic that cohesion would emerge in the community as 'different groups discovered that they faced similar problems and had similar needs'. The basis of this discovery appears to be the common experience in working-class communities of 'crime'. For 'vandalism, rape, mugging, burglary, etc. constitute just one more factor in the burdens that working-class people have to suffer'. There is no reason to believe that such a range of 'burdens' are seen by victims as being in any way similar. Just as it is probable that men from all classes see street violence as a 'problem' for them, they would not see most actions of sexual harassment as a 'problem' at all.

A further reservation about 'Left realism' stems from its misreading of the political climate within which the law and order policing debate has developed. The idea that a framework of mutual trust would lead to a situation in which the police would respond to the needs of the community and to the demands of democratic control appears to neglect the massive rift between the police and inner-city communities now extended to pit villages and towns throughout Britain. This rift has emerged from a history of deep mistrust and grudging acceptance of the police. Far from being 'Left realist', it would seem that John Lea and Jock Young have established a position based on 'democratic idealism'. Having said that, it is significant that they remark, 'it might be felt that, in fact, monitoring is about all that can be done at present'. This seems to be a much more accurate reading of the present situation.

The monitoring of operational police work is not an entirely new proposition. It has been done on specific issues by range of political, civil-rights and worker-based groups since the growth of the 'new police' in the nineteenth century. A most important recent inquiry, which had a major impact on police-community relations, was that held into the events of Southall on 23 April 1979.[10] The inquiry, held before leading academics and representatives of the black community, trade unions and the churches, set out 'to establish a full and accurate account of events in Southall . . . relating to the National Front meeting in the Town Hall, and the background to those events'. The full terms of reference raised the question of the decision to allow the National Front to march through the black community of Southall and hold an election meeting in the heart of the community. They looked at the response of the community and the presence of 'outsiders'. The central issues were, however, the decision of the police to allow the meeting, the police response to representations from local community groups, the powers and responsibilities of the police and the development of confrontation between the police and members of the public. On this latter issue concern centred on the use of police from outside the area, the role of the Special Patrol Group, the nature and extent of injuries suffered by the police and public, the circumstances in which Blair Peach – an anti-fascist demonstrator – was killed, and the procedures used by the police for the arrest and detention of suspects.

The extensive inquiry provided a searching examination, using a mass of verbal and written evidence from individuals and organizations, of the police response to the National Front march and the anti-fascist demonstration. People directly involved in the events were able to give their personal accounts in evidence to the inquiry and consequently it presented a thorough account of the events. The Unofficial Committee of Inquiry based its findings on the evidence and also provided detailed comments and recommendations.

Monitoring specific events and holding unofficial inquiries have also been developed effectively by the Welsh Council for Civil and Political Liberties (WCCPL). WCCPL's detailed investigation into 'Operation Fire' is an example of a project which developed over time and covered a wide area. Following a series of arrests and detentions without rights, allegedly in connection with the burning of second homes in Wales, WCCPL researched the cases and interviewed, through questionnaires, all of the people who had been detained. The subsequent analysis of the findings provided a closely documented account of the events and raised serious questions about the nature of the police operation.[11] This important work was extended further in 1984 with the holding of a full public inquiry 'into procedures adopted by the South Wales Constabulary and other police forces in their investigations of politically motivated offences in recent years: to consider the implications of those procedures, and to make recommendations designed to foster accountable and legitimate forms of policing in Wales.'[12]

Monitoring in this form, with the added dimension of special inquiries and reports, is also central to the development of a broader strategy. The 1984 police operations throughout Britain's pit communities provoked a range of monitoring responses. The most highly organized and systematic of these was the Sheffield Police Watch whose voluntary membership included lawyers, teachers, lecturers, community workers and others concerned with the police strategies used throughout the strike. Again through press releases, reports and a television programme,[13] Police Watch provided a thorough account of police operations, practices and behaviour based on the day-to-day monitoring of picket lines.

Unofficial inquiries or independent forms of monitoring do not carry the political weight of government backed official inquiries. They do not have the powers available to a judicial public inquiry, such as the calling of witnesses. The police reject invitations to put their case to unofficial inquiries and so evidence remains incomplete. This does not detract in any way, however, from the significance of the evidence heard. It is to their own continuing disadvantage that the police fail to contribute to such inquiries.

Other accounts of the quality of the relationship between the police and the community are typified by a most important inquiry sponsored by Bethnal Green and Stepney Trades Council in 1978.[14] The main objective of the inquiry was, by using evidence from individuals, community organizations, trade unions and others, to present evidence of racial harassment and brutality as experienced by black people in London's East End. By investigating racial attacks and cataloguing specific issues, the inquiry not only demonstrated the high level of physical attacks on black families and their property but also showed a complacency, verging on neglect, within the Metropolitan Police concerning the attacks. Important organizations, such as the Institute of Race Relations [15] and *Race Today*, have monitored this neglect and have also gone further to examine the issue of institutionalized racism within the police. The overwhelming evidence provided in these accounts, now given further support by the Policy Studies Institute report into police-community relations, has been that of police racism leading not only to neglect but also to acts of brutality.

Inquiries and interventions such as these have been useful in monitoring the state of the police. However, they remain limited since they are invariably specific to one event or one issue. What has developed more recently has been a form of longer-term monitoring of routine police operations and practices. Attempts to monitor systematically the operational practices of the police have developed with some success throughout towns and cities in the USA. The main aims of such projects were to expose malpractices previously denied by senior police officers and to provide clear evidence that existing democratic control of the police was inadequate. Following the American experience, a similar programme of police monitoring was set up in Toronto during the early 1980s as a response to official denials of police brutality and victimization towards the city's gay community.

The founding of the Citizens' Independent Review of Police Activities (CIRPA) came after a national campaign concerning a range of abuses of police power in Canada. CIRPA was established to monitor all alleged harassment, infiltration, framing and brutality by the Toronto Metropolitan Police. It consisted of representatives of all Toronto's minority groups, 'all of which have experienced police abuse in the past and have been disillusioned by existing mechanisms for dealing with it'.[16] CIRPA's main aim was to record and monitor specific cases and, where necessary, to provide legal advice and representation. Its immediate success was to force the

Attorney General to bring forward plans for a civilian review board, set up in 1982, with the explicit intention of making the Toronto Metropolitan Police more directly accountable to the people.

It was a history of similar frustrations, particularly the persistent harassment of and brutality towards black communities, which led to the Greater London Council's initiative to provide money for police monitoring throughout its boroughs. Following the return of a Labour administration in 1981, a Police Committee Support Unit was set up to provide in-depth research and advice to the GLC's Police Committee. With the Home Secretary as the police authority for the Metropolitan Police, the GLC Committee has no statutory role. The appointment of an experienced research group and legal support unit was a significant development in local government policy concerning the policing of the local community.

The Support Unit has provided thorough reports on all aspects of police work in the Greater London area and has regularly published a journal, *Policing London*. For the first time accessible and detailed information has been made available to the people of London on how they are policed and on the structure and implications of policing policy. Groups and organizations have been encouraged to apply for funding and advice to the Police Committee Support Unit so that an independent monitoring network can be established. The aim of the project is to build on the already well-established independent monitoring groups which have emerged out of earlier police-community confrontations such as Southall. Within a year at least ten monitoring groups have received GLC funding for research and resource workers. While the initial stages of a more systematic form of monitoring have lacked the consistency and cohesion of the Toronto CIRPA campaign, the overall effect of the GLC initiative has been powerful.

As is to be expected from any new initiative, particularly one so controversial, not all the groups funded by the GLC have been successful. There have been internal struggles over policy, particularly with regard to the involvement of the police, and difficulties with finance. The relationship between the groups and the Police Committee Support Unit has also not been consistent. Issues such as these, however, are often as much about individuals as about the structure of the projects. Clearly one of the most important factors in the success of monitoring is the strength of contacts with the local community – without which there can be no thorough appreciation of the problems faced by people thoughout the community. Let us look briefly at some groups which have established a coherent and successful structure for monitoring.

In May 1981, following a violent racist attack by the police on a party in Tower Hamlets, the Community Alliance for Police Accountability (CAPA) was formed. The main aims of CAPA were to inform the local community of police racism and the lack of police accountability, to organize against police racism and to work for effective accountability.[17] To do this CAPA listed five main areas of work. First, the detailed monitoring of routine policies and behaviour of all police operating in the community. Of particular concern were specific incidents relating to racial harassment or to the failure of the police to respond to complaints of racist assault and abuse. Second, the provision of a regular information service to councillors, MPs and the GLC Police Committee. Third, the provision of a 24-hour emergency service providing legal advice and support to people harassed or held by the police and to people neglected by the police. Fourth, the provision of support to people involved in legal or extra-legal action. Finally, close liaison with other monitoring groups and with the GLC Police Committee with the intention of achieving effective police accountability throughout London.

CAPA placed its main emphasis on casework while other monitoring groups prioritized campaigns and publicity. The significance of this emphasis is clear from the following extract:

> We have concentrated on talking at a local level to groups,
> youth clubs, schools, Labour Party wards, tenants,
> Councillors and to families and individuals . . . it provides
> us with the best information possible about police activities
> and attitudes.[18]

Another monitoring group, set up in 1980 after the racist murder of Akhtar Ali Baig, is the Newham Monitoring Project. The main emphasis, as with CAPA, was to 'monitor the level and extent of racist attacks in the borough and the response of the police and local authority'.[19] Again the Newham Project developed its priorities around casework, including: police racism, harassment (stop and search, detention without charge), physical abuse and violence. In the monitoring of racism and racist attacks and the lack of response by the police the Newham Project provided a 24-hour emergency service making support available to victims of racist harassment or of police racism. It monitored all routine police operations and behaviour in the borough and provided detailed information to local and national politicians and to the GLC Police Committee.

The main emphasis of these projects is on personal contact related directly to cases. Casework often leads to a commitment well beyond the cases themselves which involves the provision of further assistance and support. This intensive work, which takes project workers and volunteers into schools, youth clubs, political party meetings and, most significant of all, into people's living rooms, must be central to the success of police monitoring. More than that, however, it gives people in the community the self-confidence and technical support necessary to resist police harassment and to demand police protection. This emphasis on cases and on the provision of support to individuals has been central to the development of rape crisis centres and women's refuges for over a decade. By close monitoring of rape cases and by researching the personal experiences of women in London, Ruth Hall has provided clear evidence both of the under-reporting of rape and the lack of police co-operation, and of the frequent hostility of the police to rape victims.[20]

A further example of the successful development of monitoring by working on specific issues is the work of Inquest. Founded nationally by families and friends of people who have died in police or prison custody, or in circumstances in which police violence or neglect was alleged, Inquest gained in 1982 GLC support to monitor the holding of people in police custody in the Metropolitan force area. Again the emphasis has been on casework, particularly deaths in police custody, and on the provision of advice and legal support to the families concerned. An added dimension here has been the monitoring of the coroner's procedures for investigation and examination of cases. As a result of this important work detailed and well-researched information has been developed on an issue about which little was previously known. The gathering of this information has provided a basis for the handling of new cases.

The importance of the GLC initiative was that it enabled already existing groups to consolidate and develop their work through the provision of finance and resources. From these groups it is possible to extract the main elements which together provide the basis for successful police monitoring. First, the consistent, detailed monitoring and documenting of police policies and practices. Of particular importance here is the identification of police behaviour and attitudes as an institutionalized form rather than as the personal responses of individuals. Second, the application of pressure on the police to take action where there has been regular neglect. The priorities here have been racial violence and male violence towards women, neither of which have been taken seriously by the police. Third, the provision of practical help and support to victims of crime and also to victims of police violence or harassment. Fourth, the organization of community self-defence, which works on several levels. CAPA, for example, has assisted with private prosecutions in cases of racial violence and has also raised the issue with the local authority in order to develop strategies for dealing with racism in the community. Newham has taken a similar line and has organized pickets of pubs which provide a meeting place for known racists. Fifth, the development of accessible information and public education programmes geared to the turning of 'cases into issues'.[21] The Newham Project has been active in this and, along with other groups, has raised important questions about neighbourhood watch, community policing and the police-community liaison committees. Finally, monitoring should provide alternative accounts of events to those presented through the media by the police. This is of particular significance with regard to local papers where police viewpoints are often presented without question as 'official facts'.

The main criticism levelled against all forms of monitoring is that it takes place without police co-operation and has no formal political or legal influence over policies or priorities for operational police work. Though this is true, the informal influence and pressure which monitoring brings to bear on police work cannot be ignored. The construction and publication of alternative accounts, their coverage in the media and their submission to local and national politicians, has placed the police under considerable pressure. Having said that, the response of the police has been to criticize 'anti-police elements' and 'subversive propaganda'. It has been the case, particularly with groups such as Sheffield Police Watch, that in the initial stages the police have been helpful only to become verbally hostile once their operational policies and practices have been criticized.

Monitoring, to an extent, has been presented as a last resort to fill the gap of non-accountability. It has been argued that it should not be seen as an alternative to 'real' political accountability. Until recently, however, 'real' political accountability was taken to mean the 'triangle of accountability' which included the assumed powers of police authorities. Those assumed powers, as has been shown, are an illusion. Furthermore, it is clear that the struggles for political accountability have been lost. Monitoring is not suggested as an *alternative* to so-called democratic control of the police, but as the *only effective* means by which police operational policies and practices can be opened to public scrutiny.

Notes and references

1. 'The best police in the world'

1. All newspaper sources cited in this section are dated 30 May 1984.
2. Eyewitness accounts in J. Coulter, S. Miller and M. Walker, *State of Siege*, London Canary Press, 1984.
3. P. Smith and P. Thomas, *Striking Back*, Welsh Council for Civil and Political Liberties, 1985.
4. *Guardian*, 3 December 1984.
5. Interview with George Moores, *Diverse Reports*, Channel 4, 17 October 1984.
6. Interview with John Alderson, *ibid.*, 17 October 1984.
7. Report of the Royal Commissioners on Police Activities and Procedures, 1929.
8. Merseyside Police, publicity brochure, 1983.
9. F. Kitson, *Low Intensity Operations: Subversion, Insurgency and Counter-Insurgency*, Faber & Faber, 1971.
10. Of particular significance here is the Police and Criminal Evidence Act 1984 which will become operational in 1986.
11. M. Kettle and T. Bunyan, 'The police force of the future is now here', *New Society*, 21 August 1980, pp. 351-4.

2. The controversial tradition of the police

1. Many of these accounts are used in this chapter.
2. M. Ignatieff, 'Police and people: the birth of Mr Peel's "blue locusts" ', *New Society*, 30 August 1979, p.443.
3. P. Colquhoun, *Treatise on the Police*, publisher unknown, 1795.
4. J. Foster, *Class Struggle in the Industrial Revolution*, Methuen, 1977.
5. T.A. Critchley, *A History of the Police in England and Wales* (2nd edition), Constable, 1978.
6. E.P. Thompson, *The Making of the English Working Class*, Pelican, 1968, p. 617.
7. T.A. Critchley, *ibid.*, p.46
8. T.A. Critchley, *ibid.*, p.47
9. T.A. Critchley, *ibid.*, pp. 55-6.
10. D. Philips, *Crime and Authority in Victorian England*, Croom Helm, 1977.
11. L. Radzinowicz, *A History of English Criminal Law and Its Administration from 1750*, Vol. 4., Stevens & Sons, 1968. The relevant section, 'Towards a national standard of policing', is also contained in M. Fitzgerald *et al.*, *Crime and Society: Readings in History and Theory*, Routledge & Kegan Paul, 1981.
12. See particularly J. Stevenson, *Popular Disturbances in England*, Longman, 1979.
13. R. Storch, 'The plague of the blue locusts', *International Review of Social History*, No. 20 1975; and R. Storch, 'The policeman as domestic missionary', *Journal of Social History*, No. 9, 1975/6.

14. R. Storch, *ibid.*, 1975, p. 483.

15. R. Storch, *ibid.*, 1975, p. 485.

16. P. Cohen, 'Policing the working-class city', Fine, B. et al. (eds), *Capitalism and the Rule of Law*, Hutchinson, 1978, pp. 120-36.

17. S. Meacham, *A Life Apart: The English Working Class 1890-1914*, Thames & Hudson, 1977.

18. S. Meacham, *ibid.*, p. 18.

19. P. Cohen, *ibid.*, p. 120.

20. M. Ignatieff, *ibid.*, p. 443.

21. T. Bunyan, *The Political Police in Britain*, Quartet, 1977.

22. F.C. Mather, *Public Order in the Age of the Chartists*, Manchester University Press, 1959.

23. P. Cohen, *ibid.*, p. 132.

24. W.R. Miller, 'London's police tradition in a changing society' in S. Holdaway (ed.), *The British Police*, Edward Arnold, 1979.

25. T. Bunyan, *ibid.*, p. 66.

26. Sir Neville Macready, quoted in R. Frow, E. Frow and M. Katenka, *Strikes: a Documentary History*, Charles Knight, London, 1979.

27. T. Bowden, *Beyond the Limits of the Law*, Penguin, 1978.

28. E.J. Hobsbawm, *Industry and Empire*, Penguin, 1969, p. 193.

29. E.J. Hobsbawm, *ibid.*

30. A. Hutt, *The Post-War History of the British Working Class*, Gollancz, 1937, p. 16.

31. W. Gallacher, *Revolt on the Clyde*, Lawrence & Wishart, 1978.

32. A. Hutt, *ibid*, p. 18.

33. C.L. Mowat, *Britain Between the Wars*, Methuen, 1955, p. 126.

34. A. Hutt, *ibid.*, p. 59.

35. See C.L. Mowat, *ibid.*; R. Miliband, *Parliamentary Socialism*, Merlin, 1972; C. Farman, *The General Strike*, Panther, 1974; C. Forman, *Industrial Town: Self-Portrait of St Helens in the 1920s*, Granada/Paladin, 1979.

36. A. Hutt, *ibid.*, p. 138.

37. R. Miliband, *ibid.*, p. 136.

38. W. Paynter, *My Generation*, Allen & Unwin, 1972.

39. G.D.H. Cole and M.I. Cole, *The Condition of Britain*, Gollancz, 1937.

40. A. Hutt, *ibid.*, pp. 230-32.

41. A. Shallice, 'Remember Birkenhead: Fifty Years On', Merseyside Socialist Research Group, 1983

42. A. Shallice, *ibid.*, p. 10.

43. This account is quoted in S. Bowes, *The Police and Civil Liberties*, Lawrence & Wishart, 1966, p. 30.

44. See C.L. Mowat; S. Bowes; W. Paynter; and H. McShane *No Mean Fighter*, Pluto, 1978.

45. T. Bowden, *ibid.*, p. 229.

46. G.D.H. Cole and M.I. Cole, *ibid.*, p. 434.

47. R. Kidd, *British Liberty in Danger*, Lawrence & Wishart, 1940; F. Deegan, *There's No Other Way*, Toulouse Press, Liverpool, 1980.

48. References to Jennifer Davis's research are taken from notes on her unpublished lecture at the Open University in January 1983 entitled 'Late Nineteenth Century Policing'.

49. H. Mannheim, *Social Aspects of Crime in England Between the Wars*, Allen & Unwin, 1940.

50. V.A.C. Gattrell *et al.*, *Crime and the Law, The Social History of Crime in Western Europe since 1500*, Europa Books, 1980.

51. For further discussion see M. McIntosh, 'Changes in the organization of thieving' in S. Cohen (ed.), *Images of Deviance*, Penguin, 1971.

52. Sir P. Sillitoe, *Cloak without Dagger*, Cassell, 1955.

53. J. Patrick, *A Glasgow Gang Observed*, Eyre Methuen, 1973.

54. J. Boyle, *A Sense of Freedom*, Canongate: Edingburgh, 1977; P. Meehan, *Innocent Villain*, Pan, 1978.

55. See in particular: N. Lucas, *Britain's Gangland*, Pan, 1969; P. Gladstone-Smith, *The Crime Explosion*, MacDonald, 1970.

56. P. Meehan, *ibid.*, p. 32.

57. D. Yallop, *To Encourage the Others*, W.H. Allen, 1971, p. 22.

58. D. Hughes, quoted in S. Chibnall, *Law and Order News*, Tavistock, 1977.

59. S. Chibnall, *ibid.*

60. H. Mannheim, *Comparative Criminology*, Vol. 2, Routledge & Kegan Paul, 1965, p. 658.

61. For further accounts of this see P.P. Read, *The Train Robbers*, Allen, 1978; J. McVicar, *McVicar: By Himself*, Hutchinson, 1974.

62. J. Pearson, *The Profession of Violence*, Panther, 1973, p. 28.

63. J. L. Albini, 'Mafia as method: a comparison between Great Britain and the USA regarding the existence and structure of organized crime', *International Journal of Criminology and Penology*, 3, 1975, pp. 295-305.

64. P.P. Read, *ibid.*, p. 275.

65. For further discussion of this point see M. Kettle, 'The politics of policing and the policing of politics' in P. Hain, *Policing the Police*, Vol. 2, John Calder, 1980.

66. R. Mark, *In the Office of Constable*, Fontana, 1979.

67. D. McNee, 'Quo Vadis?', *Police Journal*, January 1980, p. 13.

68. M. O'Mahoney, *King Squealer*, Allen, 1978.

69. B. Cox, J. Shirley and M. Short, *The Fall of Scotland Yard*, Penguin, 1977.

70. P. Chippindale, 'The story of Operation Countryman', *New Statesman*, 18 January 1980.

Further reading on this chapter

T. Bunyan, *The Political Police in Britain*, Quartet, 1977; M. Brogden, *The Police: Autonomy and Consent*, Academic Press, 1982 (includes excellent primary historical material on police autonomy in Liverpool).

3. The crisis in police accountability

1. D.J. Smith and J. Gray, *Police and People in London*, Vols. I-IV. See particularly Vol. IV, 'The police in action'. Policy Studies Institute, November 1983.

2. C. Demuth, *SUS: A Report on the Vagrancy Act 1824*, The Runnymede Trust, 1978.

3. A. Brogden, ' "Sus" is dead. But what about "Sas"?', *New Community*, Spring-Summer 1981.

4. Report of the Unofficial Committee of Enquiry *Southall: 23 April 1979*, NCCL, 1980.

5. R. Mark, *In the Office of Constable*, Fontana/Collins, 1979, p. 157.

6. D. McNee, 'Quo Vadis?', *Police Journal*, January 1980, p. 10.

7. *Policing London*, April/May 1983, GLC.

8. T.A. Critchley, *A History of the Police in England and Wales* (2nd ed.), Constable, 1978, p. 300.

9. T.A. Critchley, *ibid.*, p. 301.

10. M. Banton, 'The keepers of the peace', *New Society*, 5 December 1974.

11. M. Simey, 'All dressed up and nowhere to go?', *Police*, August 1976, pp. 14-15.
12. T. Judge, 'National Police want watching locally', *Municipal Review*, 1976, pp. 236-7.
13. ACPO statement in *Police Review*, 11 July 1975.
14. Lord Denning quoted in P. Hewitt, *The Abuse of Power*, Martin Robertson, 1982.

Further reading on this chapter
It is worth following the debates on the police as covered by *State Research* Vols. 1-31. It ceased publication in 1982.

4. Misadventure on Merseyside

1. M. Kettle, '*Quis custodiet ipsos custodes*', *New Society*, 17 July 1980, pp. 128-9.
2. M. Banton, 'The keepers of the peace', *New Society*, 5 December 1974.
3. M. Brogden, 'A Police Authority – the denial of conflict', *Sociological Review* 25; 2, 1977.
4. P. Okojie and M. Noble, 'Police authorities and democratic control: a reappraisal'. Unpublished paper, Department of Law, Manchester Polytechnic.
5. J. McLure, *Spike Island: Portrait of a Police Division*, Pan Books, 1980.
6. K. Oxford, Chief Constable of Merseyside; quoted in J. McLure, *ibid.*, p. 10.
7. This quote comes from a personal interview.
8. Report of Dr J. Torry into the death of James Kelly, Wigan Health Authority 1980.
9. These statements were reported in *Newsline*, 3 October 1979.
10. *Liverpool Daily Post*, 19 October 1979.
11. *New Statesman*, 30 November 1979.
12. *Liverpool Daily Post*, 31 October 1979.
13. *Liverpool Echo*, 19 May 1980.
14. *Municipal Review*, July 1980, p. 79.
15. *The Role and Responsibilities of the Police Authority*, Report of the Working Group, Merseyside Police Committee, 22 January 1980.
16. *Guardian*, 18 April 1980.
17. *Public Disorders on Merseyside: July-August 1981*. A Report to the Police Committee by Kenneth Oxford, Chief Constable, 18 September 198' 'p. 39-40.
18. *Ibid.*, p. 22.
19. *Sunday Telegraph*, 13 September 1981.
20. For a full coverage of this see P. Scraton, 'Institutionalized racism in the Merseyside Police' in D. Cowell *et al.*, *Policing the Riots*, Junction Books, 1982, p. 24.
21. See I. Law, and J. Henfry, *A History of Race and Racism in Liverpool 1660-1950*, Liverpool Community Relations Council, 1981.
22. M. Young, *Listener*, 2 November 1978, p. 568.
23. See *Blood on the Streets*, Bethnal Green and Stepney Trades Council, 1978; 'Police Against Black People', Race and Class Pamphlet No. 6, Institute of Race Relations, 1979.
24. C. Demuth, *SUS: A Report on the Vagrancy Act 1824*, The Runnymede Trust, 1978.
25. R. Moore, *Racism and Resistance in Britain*, Pluto, 1975; A. Sivanandan, *A Different Hunger*, Pluto, 1982.
26. M. Kettle and T. Bunyan, 'The police force of the future is now here', *New Society*, 21 August 1980, pp. 351-4.
27. Unofficial Committee of Enquiry Report, *Southall: 23 April 1979*, National Council for Civil Liberties, 1980.

28. *Daily Mail*, 6 July 1981.

29. *Sunday Times*, 2 August 1981.

30. *New Society*, 9 July 1981.

31. *Daily Mail*, 6 July 1981.

32. Report to the Police Committee on the Merseyside Disorders, Chief Constable of Merseyside, Kenneth Oxford, 1981, p. 1.

33. Evidence to the Scarman Inquiry, Chief Constable of Merseyside, Kenneth Oxford, 1981, p. 6.

34. Report to Police Committee, *ibid.*, p. 2.

35. *New Statesman*, 18 September 1981.

36. *Guardian*, 6 July 1981.

37. Oxford's Evidence to Scarman, *ibid.*, p. 4.

38. Oxford's Evidence to Scarman, *ibid.*, p. 28.

39. *The Scarman Report*, para. 4. 63., HMSO, 1981, p. 64.

40. *Ibid.*, para. 2.27, p. 13.

41. Report of the Working Party on Police Public Relationships, Merseyside Police Authority, para. 3, 1. (2), October 1981.

42. *Ibid.*, para 3, 1. (3).

43. *Ibid.*, para. 3,1. (6).

44. *Ibid.*, para. 4.

45. *Ibid.*, para. 5, 5. (2).

46. *Guardian*, 10 January 1981.

47. James Jardine, former Chairman of the Police Federation quoted in *Police Review*, 20 November 1981.

48. *Guardian*, 17 March 1982.

49. 'Policing in a Democracy: Proposals for Reform' pamphlet published by Granby Ward Labour Party 1982, p.1.

50. *Ibid.*, p. 5.

5. Scarman: a diversionary interlude

1. Lord Scarman, *The Scarman Report: The Brixton Disorders 10-12 April 1981*. Cmnd. 8427, HMSO, 1981, para. 1.4, pp. 1-2. (Also published by Penguin, 1982.)

2. Lord Scarman, *ibid.*, para 1.7, p. 2.

3. Lord Scarman, *ibid.*, para 2.2, p. 11.

4. Lord Scarman, *ibid.*, para. 4. 62, p. 64.

5. J. Sim, 'Scarman: the police backlash' in M. Eve and D. Musson, *Socialist Register 1982*, Merlin, 1983.

6. S. Hall *et al.*, *Policing the Crisis*, Macmillan, 1978.

7. J. Lea and J. Young, 'The riots in Britain in 1981: urban violence and political marginalization' in D. Cowell *et al.*, *Policing the Riots*, Junction Books, 1982.

8. Community Alliance for Police Accountability, *Annual Report 1983*, Tower Hamlets.

9. *Policing London*, No. 11, 1984.

10. *Police Review*, 3 August 1979.

11. Sir D. McNee, *Sunday Mirror*, 7 November 1982.

12. D.J. Smith and J. Gray, *Police and People in London: IV The police in action*, Policy Studies Institute, 1983.

Further reading on this chapter
'From Resistance to Rebellion', *Race and Class*, Vol. XXIII, 2/3, 1982; A. Sivanandan, *A Different Hunger*, Pluto, 1982; P. Gordon, *White Law*, Pluto, 1983;

The Policy Studies Institute Report, *Police and People in London*, November 1983, Vols. I-IV; Centre for Contemporary Cultural Studies, *The Empire Strikes Back*, Hutchinson, 1982.

6. Can you feel the force?

1. J. Straw, 'Wanted: A firm hand on the police', *Guardian*, 21 April 1980.
2. G.J. Dear, 'Law and Order: the way ahead', *Police Journal*, January 1980, pp. 60-71
3. J. Anderton, 'Accountability', *Police Review*, 6 February 1981, pp. 208-9.
4. Sir R. Mark, *In the Office of Constable*, Fontana/Collins, 1979.
5. D. McNee, 'Quo Vadis', *Police Journal*, January 1980.
6. D. McNee, 'Street Riots', *Sunday Mirror*, 31 October 1982.
7. M. Kettle, 'The politics of policing and the policing of politics' in P. Hain (ed.), *Policing the Police*, Vol. II, John Calder, 1980.
8. E.P. Thompson, *Writing by Candlelight*, Merlin, 1980.
9. E. St Johnston, 'Opinion among the police has moved towards a national police force controlled by the Home Secretary', *Guardian Agenda*, 10 August 1981.
10. J. Alderson, *Policing Freedom*, McDonald & Evans, 1979.
11. 'Policing together: an introduction to community policing', *Devon and Cornwall Constabulary Information Series*, 1980.
12. Home Office Circular, 'Police and Coloured Communities', Home Office, 1967.
13. *Guardian*, 13 October 1981.
14. *Sunday Times*, 17 January 1982.
15. *Times Educational Supplement*, 18 September 1981.
16. *Guardian*, 19 March 1981 and *New Statesman*, 27 March 1981.
17. This incident was recalled in an interview with the head teacher of a large Milton Keynes comprehensive school in June 1983.
18. R. Baldwin and R. Kinsey, *Police Powers and Politics*, Quartet, 1982, p. 101.
19. Lord Scarman, *ibid.*, para 6. 24., p. 106.
20. K. Newman, 'The Urban Future', Inner City Conference speech at Bramshill, September 1982.
21. R. Baldwin and R. Kinsey, *ibid.*, p. 288.
22. *Policing London*, 8, 1983, pp. 3-4.
23. *Hansard*, 29 February 1984.
24. *Policing London*, 14, 1984, p. 113.
25. *Hansard*, 19 July 1984: reply by Douglas Hurd.
26. *Policing London*, *ibid.* p. 113.
27. *Guardian*, 1 March 1983.

Further reading on this chapter
C. Ackroyd *et al.*, *The Technology of Political Control*, (2nd edn), Pluto, 1981; *Policing London*, Vol. I onwards, GLC, 1982-continues; P. Gordon, 'Community Policing', *Critical Social Policy*, Summer 1983.

7. A national police force?

1. *Observer*, 23 October 1977.
2. S. Hall *et al.*, *Policing The Crisis*, Macmillan, 1978, p. 283.
3. A. Scargill, quoted in *New Left Review*, July/August 1975.
4. Maurice Macmillan, quoted in D. Warren, *Shrewsbury: Whose Conspiracy?*, New Park Publications, 1980, p. 10.

5. Quoted in P. Smith and P. Thomas, 'The history of Orgreave', unpublished mss., Cardiff 1984.

6. J. Dromey and G. Taylor, *Grunwick: The Workers' Story*, Lawrence & Wishart, 1978.

7. Sir R. Mark, *In the Office of Constable*, Fontana/Collins, 1979, p. 317.

8. Sir R. Mark, *ibid*, p. 160.

9. Speech made at the University of Birmingham 3 March 1978, quoted in *State Research* No. 5, April-May 1978.

10. R. Reiner, 'Police and picketing', *New Society*, 7 July 1977.

11. K. Sloan, *Police Review*, 9 February 1979.

12. P. Hewitt, 'Our right to demonstrate', *Rights*, Vol. 4, No. 6, NCCL, 1980.

13. James Anderton, Chief Constable of Greater Manchester, quoted in the *Guardian*, 10 January 1981.

14. Lancashire Trades Council Association's Observer; reports on the events of 29 November 1983.

15. Lord Denning; statement on *Diverse Reports*, Channel 4, 1984.

16. Peter Hennessy of the Policy Studies Institute in an interview for *Diverse Reports*, Channel 4, 1984.

17. Charles McLachlan, Chief Constable of Nottinghamshire and ACPO President in a television interview in 1984.

18. *Sunday Times*, 20 May 1984.

19. *Policing London*, 13, 1984, p. 78.

20. *Guardian*, 23 June 1984.

21. *Newsnight Special*, BBC2, December 1984.

22. *File on Four*, BBC Radio 4, 31 August 1984.

23. George Moores, Chair of South Yorkshire Police Committee, *Diverse Reports*, Channel 4, 1984.

24. C. Bateman, 'The dictatorship of the 43 chief constables', *Guardian*, 11 August 1984.

25. See *Policing London*, 13, 1984, p. 78 for further figures. By June 1984 the Association of County Councils estimated their additional costs for policing at £60 million.

26. Margaret Simey in C. Bateman, *ibid*.

27. *Ibid*.

28. *Ibid*.

29. *Ibid*.

30. Gabrielle Cox in C. Bateman, *ibid*.

31. *Police Review* 20, July 1984.

32. Interview on *Taking Liberties*, BBC2, November 1984.

33. S. Gregson-Murray, *LAG Bulletin*, August 1984.

34. *Guardian*, 26 November 1984.

35. *Guardian*, 26 November 1984.

Further reading on this chapter
S. Hall *et al.*, *Policing the Crisis*, Macmillan, 1978; J. Coulter, S. Miller and M. Walker, *State of Siege*, Canary Press, 1984; B. Fine and R. Millar (eds), *Policing the Miners*, Lawrence & Wishart, 1985; P. Smith and P. Thomas, *Striking Back*, WCCPL, 1985.

8. Responding to the state of the police

1. C. Bateman 'The dictatorship of the 43 chief constables', *Guardian*, 11 August 1984.

2. *Guardian* 13 August 1984.

3. *Guardian* 14 August 1984.

4. See D. Cowell *et al.*, *Policing the Riots*, Junction Books, 1982; P. Scraton, *Controversies Around Police Powers and Accountability*, Open University Press, Milton Keynes, 1982.

5. Letter to the *Guardian*, 31 December 1983.

6. R. Baldwin and R. Kinsey, *Police Powers and Politics*, Quartet, 1983.

7. J. Lea and J. Young, *What is to be done abou Law and Order?*, Penguin, 1984.

8. J. Lea and J. Young, *ibid.* p. 258.

9. J. Lea and J. Young, *ibid.* p. 260.

10. Report of the Unofficial Committee of Inquiry, *Southall: 23 April 1979*, NCCL, 1980.

11. Welsh Council for Civil and Political Liberties, *Operation Fire*, WCCPL, 1980; P. Smith, 'Detention without rights' in P. Scraton and P. Gordon, *Causes for Concern*, Penguin, 1984.

12. J. Davies, Lord Gifford and T. Richards, *Political Policing in Wales*, WCCPL, 1984.

13. *Taking Liberties*, BBC2, November 1984.

14. Bethnal Green and Stepney Trade Council, *Blood on the Streets*, BGSTC, 1978.

15. Institute of Race Relations, 'Police Against Black People, Race and Class Pamphlet No.6, 1979. Also important here has been the publication *Race Today*.

16. CIRPA Information Document, Toronto, 1982.

17. Community Alliance for Police Accountability *Annual Report*, Tower Hamlets, 1983.

18. *Ibid.*, p. 4.

19. Newham Monitoring Project Report, Newham, 1983, p. 2.

20. R. Hall, *Ask Any Woman*, Falling Wall Press, 1985.

21. A. Sivanandan, 'Challenging racism: strategies for the 1980s', *Race and Class*, Vol. XXV, No 2.